DESMOND LESLIE
(1921–2001)

DESMOND LESLIE
(1921–2001)

THE BIOGRAPHY OF AN IRISH GENTLEMAN

ROBERT O'BYRNE

THE LILLIPUT PRESS
DUBLIN

First published 2010 by
THE LILLIPUT PRESS
62–63 Sitric Road, Arbour Hill
Dublin 7, Ireland
www.lilliputpress.ie

ISBN   978 1 84351 163 2

1 3 5 7 9 10 8 6 4 2

Set in 11.5 pt on 16 pt Electra by Marsha Swan
Printed in England by MPG Books Ltd, Cornwall

DESMOND LESLIE
(1921–2001)

ONE

SOME YEARS BEFORE Desmond Leslie's death in February 2001, a guidebook to Ireland chose to describe his family as 'mildly eccentric'. He took umbrage at this portrayal and wrote to the publishers informing them that, on the contrary, the Leslies were 'very eccentric'. The text was accordingly amended – and with good reason. Though the family has lived in Ireland for over three and a half centuries, it has a much older lineage and can claim Attila the Hun as an ancestor, as well as Native American blood. The first of their number to settle in this country was equally bellicose, despite becoming a clergyman. John Leslie moved from Scotland to Ireland in 1633 after being appointed Bishop of Raphoe; later he became Bishop of Clogher since this diocese was located closer to Dublin. He is remembered as 'the Fighting Bishop' who at the age of sixty-seven married eighteen-year-old Catherine Cunningham and managed to father eight children before dying just weeks short of his hundredth birthday.

By then he had bought Glaslough Castle and demesne in County Monaghan. It has remained the Leslie home ever since, although the family acquired a great deal of property elsewhere too; in the late nineteenth century they owned close to 50,000 acres spread across seven counties. The wealth generated by this land permitted them to be indifferent to public opinion and to find themselves endlessly interesting. Dean Swift wrote various squibs about the Leslies including the following lines:

> Here I am in Castle Leslie
> With Rows and Rows of Books upon the Shelves
> Written by the Leslies
> All about Themselves.

Charles Powell Leslie, who inherited the estate in 1743, was sufficiently independent to be one of the very few great Irish landlords to refuse the offer of a peerage from the British government in return for voting for the Act of Union in 1800. Unfortunately he was unable to enjoy this distinction for long since he died the same year.

And so it continued to the twentieth century, with each generation outdoing the last in unconventionality. The Leslies have always been inclined to shock other people but rarely themselves. For example, none of the family displayed any surprise when Lionel Leslie, who at the end of the First World War had announced his intention to walk all the way home from India (and subsequently tried to cross Africa on foot accompanied by a Masai warrior), should later in life, while resident on the Scottish Isle of Mull, have cherished an unwavering belief in the Loch Ness Monster. In fact, he was confident the loch contained a number of such creatures and devoted much time and energy to proving their existence, albeit without success. Meanwhile his brother Seymour once wrote an avant-garde novel called *The Silent Queen*, about an American millionaire who invents a noiseless lavatory, and later became a highly successful fundraiser for Queen Charlotte's Hospital in London.

But Lionel and Seymour's older brother was unquestionably the most idiosyncratic of the siblings. Born in 1885, John Leslie received an upbringing typical of his class and era, including a period at Eton College, which he claimed to dislike, but persistently visited as an adult, followed by time as an undergraduate at King's College, Cambridge. Afterwards, unexpectedly, he underwent a conversion both to Roman Catholicism and Irish nationalism, asked to be addressed in future as Shane and renounced his birthright, Castle Leslie. He took to wearing his own interpretation of traditional Irish costume (it involved a saffron-coloured kilt and a cloak), briefly considered the priesthood and offended his Unionist parents by standing as a Nationalist in Derry during the 1910 British general election. Unsuccessful in this attempt, he subsequently travelled to the United States where he met William Bourke Cockran, a friend of his first cousin Winston Churchill (their American-born mothers were sisters). Considered the most brilliant orator of his generation, Bourke Cockran had been born in County Sligo but at the age of seventeen emigrated to New York where he became a successful barrister before his election to Congress as a Democrat (and is credited with teaching Churchill how to speak in public).

It was while staying with Bourke Cockran on Long Island that Shane Leslie met the former's sister-in-law Marjorie Ide. Her background was almost as colourful as his own. Marjorie's father, Henry Clay Ide, had grown up in relative poverty in Vermont before he, like William Bourke Cockran, became a lawyer and then a judge. Following his wife's early death, he was appointed Chief Justice of Samoa and travelled there with his daughters, who befriended another western resident on the island, the writer Robert Louis Stevenson. Judge Ide next became Governor General of the Philippines and for four years Marjorie, the youngest of his children, acted as her father's hostess and reputedly saved the old walls of Manila from being torn down.

Shane Leslie in his Irish kilt c.1960s.
Photograph by Antony Armstrong-Jones, later Lord Snowdon.

She and her sister Anne paid a State visit to China on behalf of the American government and while in Beijing met the Empress-Dowager who presented them with gold rings and jade bracelets as souvenirs. Later, when Judge Ide was sent to Madrid as US Ambassador to Spain, Marjorie went there too but in 1912 she returned home to stay with her older sister Anne, by this date married to the much older William Bourke Cockran. Here Marjorie was introduced to Shane Leslie, four years her junior, a Catholic convert who had given up his inheritance and intended to make a living as a writer. But Shane was also witty, good-looking and charming and these attractive qualities overcame his potential disadvantages. In June 1912, the couple were married in the conservatory of the Bourke Cockrans' home before sailing to Madrid for their honeymoon and then on to London where they were to live until the outbreak of the First World War.

Shane and Marjorie's first child, the future writer Anita Leslie, was born in November 1914. Given that war with Germany had already been declared, mother and baby, along with sundry servants, soon crossed the Atlantic to take sanctuary in the Bourke Cockran home. Shane, meanwhile, joined the British forces after the death of his younger brother Norman (to whom, following Shane's renunciation, Castle Leslie was supposed to pass). He saw service briefly in Gallipoli and then the Dardanelles before ill health forced him to leave the army. Like his wife he travelled to the United States where he was attached to the British embassy in Washington, working with the ambassador, Sir Cecil Arthur Spring-Rice, to soften Irish-American hostility towards England and to convince the American government of the urgency of joining the Allies against Germany. Shane and Marjorie's second child, a boy christened John but always known as Jack, was born in New York in December 1916; given that Shane had renounced his right to Castle Leslie and Norman had been killed, Jack was now declared heir to the family estate.

Marjorie Leslie in her wedding dress, 1912.

Shane and Marjorie together with their two children eventually returned to Europe in 1919. Because of Ireland's political instability, they only spent the summer at Castle Leslie over the next few years but based themselves in London, initially at 10 Talbot Square near Hyde Park. In 1922 they moved to 12 Westbourne Terrace, which would be their home until just before the outbreak of the Second World War. It was in London that the couple's third child, Desmond Peter Arthur Leslie, was born by caesarean section at the Hospital of St John and Elisabeth, St John's Road, at 9.20 am on Wednesday, 29 June 1921. Both his elder siblings would remember the occasion. They were at home in the top-floor nursery when the cook, Mrs Carr, announced from the kitchen through a speaking tube, 'A baby brother for Master Jacky.' Anita thought it very unfair that the new arrival was only for her brother.

Within the hour another announcement came up to the nursery: the new baby's great-aunt, thrice-married Jennie Churchill, had died at almost exactly the same moment the baby had been born. Staying with friends in Somerset some weeks before, she had fallen downstairs and broken her ankle. Gangrene set in, her left leg was amputated and while lying in bed on that morning in late June, she remarked to her maid, 'Mrs Leslie's operation is just over. I wonder what the baby is.' Then she added, 'The hot water bottle has burst,' lay back on the pillows and soon afterwards died; in fact, an artery in her thigh had haemorrhaged. Afterwards her older son Winston commented, 'As one leaves this world, another arrives in it,' an observation especially applicable to Desmond Leslie who believed that all our lives follow intertwined cycles. But perhaps too he had always been intended to take Jennie Churchill's place on Earth, since the pair of them had so much in common, both possessing the same lively intelligence, enormous curiosity, exceptional charm and physical appeal.

Desmond was christened three weeks after his birth. Among his godparents was Prince Arthur, the Duke of Connaught, Queen

Victoria's youngest child and an intimate friend of his grandmother Leonie Leslie. The Duke's own godfather had been the first Duke of Wellington and Desmond used to say that in this way he had a direct link with the Battle of Waterloo and the defeat of Napoleon. In fact, an earlier member of the Leslie family had paid for the education of the future Duke of Wellington (to whom he was connected by marriage), allowing Desmond to observe that Waterloo had actually been won on the playing fields of Glaslough. The Duke's bridle still remains in Castle Leslie. A kindly but somewhat ineffectual man, the Duke of Connaught was popularly known as the Duke of Cannot. He was often invited to stay at Castle Leslie where on one occasion a footman hired for the ducal visit became drunk and burst into the dining room to declare, 'Your Royal Highness, I'll have you know we're so loyal in Portadown, we're still mourning your mum.' Queen Victoria had, by this date, been dead for many years. Although by then elderly (he had been born in 1850), the Duke sometimes invited Desmond to his London residence, Clarence House, where his godson would entertain him by playing the piano.

The other godparents were Countess Beatty and Evan Morgan. Like Marjorie Leslie, Ethel Beatty was an American heiress, the only daughter of Chicago department-store magnate Marshall Field. Following a divorce from her first husband, she married David, Earl Beatty, who in 1919 had been appointed Admiral of the British Fleet, serving as First Sea Lord for the next eight years. His family being Irish, among Earl Beatty's other titles was that of Viscount Borodale of Wexford.

As for Evan Morgan, who on the death of his father in 1934 became second Viscount Tredegar, he was one of the most extraordinary characters in Britain between the two world wars. An aesthete, poet and novelist, among his wide circle of friends were H.G. Wells, Aldous Huxley, Augustus John, Nancy Cunard and Ivor

Desmond as a young child.

Novello. He maintained a menagerie at his family home in Wales, including bears, baboons and kangaroos, with one of which, called Somerset, he would box. He had a particular affinity for birds, probably derived from his mother who was rumoured to have built nests large enough for her to perch inside. His favourite parrot, Blue Boy, was trained to crawl up Evan Morgan's trouser leg and then peep out through his open fly buttons. Though twice married, like Shane Leslie he was a Catholic convert and managed to combine holding the position of Privy Chamberlain of Cape and Sword to Popes Benedict XV and Pius XI with a passion for black magic; he and the notorious satanist Aleister Crowley – who called Tredegar the 'Adept of Adepts' – held strange voodoo rituals at Tredegar House. But both at the time of the christening and until his death twenty-eight years later, he proved a good godfather to Desmond Leslie, presenting him on that first occasion with a Charles II plate and cup.

Other christening gifts included a large silver jug from the Duke of Connaught, a Queen Anne silver cup from Countess Beatty, a gold rosary from his grandmother, Leonie Leslie, and a silver knife, fork and spoon from his aunt Anne Bourke Cockran.

At the age of four months, Desmond made his first trip overseas, travelling with his mother and siblings first to Paris and thence to San Remo where they spent the winter before returning to London in April 1922. This journey set a pattern for the years ahead; Marjorie was a restless, unsettled individual and rarely stayed too long in any place. Sometimes she took one or more of her children with her, sometimes she left them in a variety of schools or with different guardians. As Anita Leslie would comment, 'In my parents' view schools performed the same function that kennels did for dogs. They were places where pets could be conveniently deposited while their owners travelled.' At least in part, Marjorie's peripatetic habit can be interpreted as an escape from the problems that soon arose in her marriage.

Anita with Jack and Desmond as boys, late 1920s. Jack is on the left.

Like his father before him – and his younger son after – Shane
Leslie was not a faithful husband. 'They were wonderfully unsuited,'
Desmond once commented of his parents, calling them 'a most
unlikely couple'. His sister Anita's elegant memoir *The Gilt and the
Gingerbread* makes it plain that Shane and Marjorie soon drifted apart
and that on more than one occasion the latter considered leaving her
husband for good. However, after their marriage she had followed
his example and become a Roman Catholic, thereby making divorce
impossible. Moreover her mother-in-law Leonie was appalled at the
very idea of divorce (even though her own beloved sister Jennie had
been a divorcée) and, as Anita writes, 'had formed the opinion that
the most uncongenial temperaments could adjust as soldiers do to

enforced companionship'. So Marjorie and Shane remained married but with increased frequency lived for long periods apart.

This meant that while young the children did not see a great deal of their father. In any case, Shane Leslie was temperamentally disinclined to be a devoted parent. In this respect, once again, he was following the example of his own father who, when each of his four sons was born, had only observed, 'Another damned boy!' and then took no further interest in their upbringing. Anita Leslie recalled how, on the boat journey back from the United States in 1919, she and Jack were almost unaware that Shane was on the same crossing since not once did he come near the pair of them. He never gave his children presents or remembered their birthdays or even embraced them. 'I think we realized fairly early,' Anita later wrote, 'that our father did not exactly dislike us – he would merely have preferred us not to have been born.' She noted that during her childhood, 'the women of the family dominated us'. It's telling that in *Pardon My Return*, Desmond's 1946 novel largely set in a fictional equivalent of Castle Leslie called Cruiskeen, women dominate the household. The father of his protagonist in the book, Rory Headstone, has died many years before the story begins and Cruiskeen is run by a grandmother, mother and two spinster aunts.

Even when physically present, Shane Leslie could be emotionally absent. Although universally known as an amusing and highly intelligent conversationalist and much in demand socially, he rarely addressed a remark to his own offspring and would sit through meals with them in complete silence. Still worse, 'If we ventured an opinion,' Anita remembered, her father's eyes 'would close like those of a parrot – the bottom lid moving upwards.' 'As a child and through my early years,' Desmond wrote in 1965, 'I was always made to feel inadequate, a sort of moron who was tolerated because "Poor Desmond can't help it." Naturally this took a lot of living down.' Even when they reached adulthood, Shane Leslie still displayed no interest in his children, only ever speaking to them if they spoke to him first.

With both parents so often away from home, Desmond's closest bond while young was with his nanny Ethel Weston, always known as Nanny Weston, who looked after him until he was sixteen and to whom he remained devoted for the rest of his life. Evidently the feeling was mutual; baby Desmond had blond hair, which remained a pale gold long after it should have grown darker. Marjorie eventually discovered that Nanny Weston had been carefully dyeing her little charge's locks. Desmond's daughter Antonia remembers being told of an episode when Marjorie in typically impulsive fashion decided to take her children to France but to leave Ethel Weston behind; Desmond, then aged perhaps five or six, became hysterical and wet himself, only finding solace when finally reunited with his nanny.

Desmond as a little boy with teddy, early 1920s.

Shortly before his marriage to Agnes Bernelle in 1945, he wrote to his father insisting that 'Nanny has been summoned and must sit in the family pew at the wedding along with the rest of us.' And when she died in September 1972, he told his sister Anita that he had Nanny Weston to thank 'for a calm and happy childhood'. She had been, he said, 'one of those rare simple really good people who more than deserve her reward ... Dear Nanny, such a blessed person without a single blemish of character.'

One other constant in Desmond's early life was Castle Leslie. Although Shane was no longer the estate's intended heir, he was still his parents' eldest son and so, once peace had been re-established in Ireland, he and his family would regularly spend time in County Monaghan, especially during the summer months. Castle Leslie lay immediately on the southern side of the border created by the Anglo-Irish Treaty of 1921, which meant the Leslies were cut off from many of their old neighbours – families like the Caledons and the Stronges who lived only a few miles away. But as much as possible, the pre-war style of life was maintained by Desmond's grandparents, Sir John – known as Papa Jack – and his wife Leonie. Although the once vast Leslie estate had shrunk owing to sales conducted through the Land Commission, the old demesne, which ran to more than 1500 acres, was still intact and proved a wonderful playground for Shane and Marjorie's three children. There were still plenty of servants in the house and gardeners looking after the grounds; grooms in the stable and friendly relations with the residents of Glaslough, the village lying immediately outside Castle Leslie's gates. 'We felt we belonged here,' Anita once wrote. 'We belonged to this earth, to these trees, to this rushy lake. We were part of the landscape.'

Interviewed by his daughter Sammy a few years before he died, Desmond recalled a childhood in which Castle Leslie represented 'pure magic. There was the smell of porridge and the sound of jackdaws in the chimneys and that marvellous lake out

View of Castle Leslie.

front. The worst thing was going away back to horrid old London; how nasty it smelled of oil and tar.' At the little local railway station in Glaslough, he and his brother and sister were allowed to drive the shunting locomotive up and down the line when no trains were due and to work the signal box and the level crossing. Meanwhile, within rambling Castle Leslie there were boundless rooms in which young children could explore and play, and conceal themselves should this be necessary. 'There were huge attics to hide in when the adults wanted one to do something boring like brush one's teeth, and a wonderful basement to look for ghosts.' Castle Leslie also offered opportunities for the children to make mischief, such as the occasion when a grand house party was disrupted by each bedroom being booby-trapped. When the French ambassador opened his door, for example, a motor horn was rigged to go off, while one woman suffered a collapse when she discovered an eerie grey hand emerging from between her pillows; it was a wooden model used for stretching gloves.

Leonie Leslie's sociability and wide circle of friends meant the house was often full of guests, among them Prince Pierre of Monaco who, following an acrimonious divorce from Princess Charlotte Louise in 1929, had been banished from the principality by his father-in-law. Prince Pierre thereafter spent much time in England with his son, the future Prince Rainier III, who would also regularly come to stay at Castle Leslie. Two years younger than Desmond, on one occasion Rainier joined him in a chemical experiment that led to a loud explosion and equally noisy complaints from everyone else in the house. It was by no means the last time that Desmond's behaviour at Castle Leslie would cause a stir.

Painting of the Leslie children, Jack, Anita and Desmond, by Stanley Mercer, 1932.

T
W
O

EVENTUALLY THE TIME CAME for Desmond to go away to
school. His formal education had begun at Mr Gladstone's, a pre-
paratory school in Knightsbridge to which he was taken daily, and
from which collected, by Nanny Weston. Then he was sent to board
at Ladycross, a Catholic prep school near Seaford on the Sussex
coast run by a couple called Mr and Mrs Roper. At thirteen, he
moved on to public school. Although Shane had attended Eton,
he decided his two sons should go elsewhere; in her memoir, Anita
rather slyly suggested her father didn't want to be upstaged at his old
alma mater by the next generation of Leslies, but the fact that Shane
was a Catholic probably also influenced his choice. Jack had been
sent to Downside Abbey, the Benedictine public school in Somerset
where he was not very happy, so Desmond went to Ampleforth, a
similar establishment in Yorkshire, which suited his temperament

rather better. One reason for this was the character of the monk running his house, St Dunstan's, which had recently been established.

Then a relatively young man, Fr Oswald Vanheems would also be housemaster to Desmond's own two sons Sean and Mark when they attended Ampleforth in the 1960s. Fr Oswald, affectionately known by the boys under his care as Ozzy, seems to have become a surrogate father for Desmond, someone far more attuned to his personality than was the remote Shane Leslie. Thirty years after leaving Ampleforth, Desmond was still in touch with his former housemaster, visiting him just a week before the latter died. Subsequently Desmond wrote to Shane that the old monk had been 'one of those simple good people who manage to retain a sort of heavenly innocence throughout life, which is so rare nowadays. I think Heaven got jealous and took him to where his qualities would be more appreciated.' Fr Oswald also held his former charge in great affection; Desmond's younger son Mark remembers the monk turning up at the family home in London and acting as peacemaker whenever his parents were going through a particularly difficult patch in their often stormy marriage. The other Ampleforth monk who left a lasting mark on Desmond was Fr Aelred Graham, a deeply spiritual man who encouraged what would be a lifelong interest in mysticism and global religions. It was Fr Aelred who conducted the service at Desmond and Agnes Bernelle's wedding in 1945.

Among Desmond's contemporaries at Ampleforth was a young man called George Hume, better known as Basil Hume after his appointment in February 1976 to the position of Roman Catholic Archbishop of Westminster. At the time Desmond wrote a congratulatory letter to his old school friend remarking,

> Can't you just see Ozzy on Cloud Nine giggling with delight? I can't think of anything that would please him more. Now I suppose I must resist all tempting offers from Sunday papers for meaningless memoirs when we were bed-neighbours in the

North Dormitory. I recall filling your po with Eno's one night to your consternation. What a nice child I was.

Another letter to Hume, written nine years later, had a more serious tone and concerned the Catholic Church's rejection of contraception even within marriage. 'What is the real, deep, underlying reason for this inflexibility?' Desmond asked the Archbishop, who by then had been made a cardinal.

Pope John Paul II, Desmond wrote,

says that husbands should not lust after their wives. Well, if they don't lust after their own wives, they're going to start lusting after someone else's wife. That's for sure. Good husbands are a lusty breed of men. Ask any wife who has a sparkle in her eye and an aura of calm and contentment. Would he wish to destroy that?

Marital lustiness was unlikely to have been among Desmond's concerns while at Ampleforth, where he was more engaged with the usual boyish interests of sport and clubs, as is shown by a cache of letters written to his parents (and, in the early years, also addressed to Nanny Weston) and always signed 'love from your devoted Des'. 'I have joined several societies this term,' he told them on one occasion, 'including the Musical, the Railway, the Scientific and the Senior Debate.' There were reports of typical practical jokes, such as the time one of the boys emptied a tin of salts into the biology-room fish tank 'and when the fauna within were hauled out for our inspection it was found all the wretched waterbugs, tadpoles and little fishes had a violent attack of dyrroehia (if that's how you spell it) which hardly added to the general advancement of us scholars'. Inevitably at that age food was another subject of abiding fascination and one letter announced that 'this morning the porridge had fermented and it stunk out the whole refectory building. Everything from floor polish to the cook's cat were blamed until the porridge was found responsible.'

Shane and Marjorie in middle age at Castle Leslie.

Anita and Jack drove up from London to spend a weekend with their brother after he had carefully budgeted how much their visit would cost ('There, just see what offspring prodigy can do!!' he informed Marjorie). The trip was deemed a great success and afterwards he told his parents: 'We had such a lovely weekend, glorious weather, grand entertainment and lots of fun', which left him so exhausted that 'I slumbered the whole of Tuesday's lessons, but I think I am working hard now I feel less soporific.'

As he grew older, Desmond often went on long walking tours across the Yorkshire Moors. 'Tomorrow evening,' he informed Shane and Marjorie, 'I am going off with another boy with provisions and a tent, and we will camp out, then the next day we will hike around and come back in the evening. This is our scout journey, it will be rather fun.' One trip he didn't tell his parents about took place on the school's annual moors expedition, an event known as Goremire Day. Everyone at Ampleforth was required to join the outing and to travel either on foot or by vehicle provided this was not powered by internal combustion – in other words was a bicycle. Desmond managed to get round the rule by hiring a steam traction engine, which, as he pointed out, depended on external combustion. He duly drove this to the destination on Goremire Day.

Desmond (back) and traction engine at Ampleforth.

These early letters show the emergence and development of Desmond's creative talents. He was a keen musician and excellent pianist and once wrote to his mother in London, 'I'm afraid I shall be of exceeding rage if you were to sell my beloved piano. It is so nice, and gives me something to do when at a dead end for occupation.' Desmond's earliest music teacher was his grandmother Leonie, whose circle of friends had included Richard Wagner's widow Cosima. Taught by the Hungarian composer and player Stephen Heller, both Leonie and her sister Jennie had been brilliant pianists; when the latter first met her parents-in-law, the Duke and Duchess of Marlborough, at Blenheim Palace, she dazzled them with a piano recital. As Anita Leslie later wrote, 'Even the Churchills knew it must be good because so many notes were being struck at the same time.' At Castle Leslie, Leonie's Bechstein grand piano in the drawing room had been chosen for her by the famous Polish musician Paderewski and it was on this instrument that Desmond used to practise as a child. His first proper music teacher, he once wrote,

an august and splendid white-haired lady, was horrified when I showed her a much more exciting sound could be produced from the piano by opening the lid and hitting the strings with a hammer. At Ampleforth I made the interesting experiment of re-arranging some of the pipes in the organ loft by switching pairs a semitone apart one Saturday evening. The results on Sunday in the Abbey Church were most interesting.

Desmond's performing abilities were also displayed in other ways. 'Last night,' he told his parents in one letter from Ampleforth,

our house and two others produced their shows. I had to produce ours and it was a complete success, and everyone said it was the best. Our prize number was the school doctor (me) doing an operation … It was the hit of the evening and someone said they wished St Dunstan's partook of every entertainment. I thoroughly enjoyed producing and acting in it. It was all great fun.

At the age of fifteen, he converted a former footmen's room in one wing of Castle Leslie into a little theatre. At the rear of this he installed a colour projector that could throw light patterns and scenic changes on to the stage in time to music from a Panatrope, the world's first electric record player. 'The Ride of the Walkure was my crowning achievement,' he later remembered. 'With Walkure on black chargers actually scudding through banks of moving storm clouds and disappearing into the mists. Wotan's Farewell filled the end wall with projected flames and clouds of smoke.' Unfortunately the castle's generator could not cope 'and finally packed up plunging the house and my irate grandparents into total darkness'.

Desmond now started to write short plays for performance by puppets in his theatre, usually amusing skits featuring people from the neighbourhood. In her memoirs, Anita remembered one such piece intended to entertain the brothers of Erik, Earl of Caledon who lived just across the border from Castle Leslie; it concluded with the lines 'Hush, hush, whisper who dares? Little Earl Erik is saying his prayers.'

'Just finished the first copy of a comedy for production at Glaslough,' a letter from Ampleforth informed Shane and Marjorie, 'it is rather spectacular but not quite as personal as the other scurrilities we produced.' One of those 'other scurrilities' has survived, a satire in rhyming couplets on the annual charity fete held in the grounds of Castle Leslie. An early scene features many members of the family:

Enter Lady Leslie.
'Why doesn't someone man the boats? And where are Jack and Nita?
If only I had Winston here, I wouldn't be dead-beat-ah!
Marjorie! Why don't you go and greet that Mrs Strong!
I'll have to get that chair myself, as Bryce will take so long.

Tell Papa Jack to come right back, and not to leave the tennis,
And give him this brown ditty-bag in which to count his
pennies.'

Nanny walks by, singing,
'Oh kind folks, Buy a ticket! Oh! Won't you have a try?
Oh! Please do take a chance – it is for charitye!
There are only a thousand tickets, and I am the only seller,
And if you win, you'll proudly own a blue cotton umbrella.'

All buy tickets, and Nanny goes off.
Enter Lord Belmore. Leonie greets him and says,
'Oh, how do you do, dear Lord Belmore, how kind of you to
come.
We've every kind of thing to sell, I'm sure you will buy some.
There's beads and socks – and bibs and smocks
And soap – and nice tea cosies
Jumpers and frocks and ancient stocks
High rabbits and dead rosies!
But best of all, I think for you, is this wee pink, woolly hood,
You say you have no use for it, but you should, dear man, you
should!'

Lord Belmore, looking about,
'Hum-ah! Let's see – I'll take those buns and buy that ten
pound cake
I'll have that pie, and the rabbits high, my hunger for to slake.
But best of all, dear Lady L, I'll take you now to tea.
For only a shilling, I'll get a good filling,
Enough in fact for three!'

Jack saunters by, singing,
'I am the family dandy – I am the girls' delight!
With my trousers creased and my hair well-greased
I am making the fete more bright.
But the day to me is one of flats
For the Countess of Caledon can't see my spats!'

Enter Anita,
'While Jack was with the peacocks playing
And his straw hat proudly displaying
Desmond and I made nearly a pound
Rowing the children round and round.
We'd take them out, and tip the boat
And tell them that it wouldn't float
Then they'd beg to go ashore, for their mothers begin to roar
So, to bring them back, we charged them double
And saved ourselves a lot of trouble!
Now none of you will ever dare, to tell me to go and comb my hair!'

Apparently Desmond's enthusiasm for the theatre began to make Marjorie anxious as she considered her youngest child's future career because he had to write and reassure her that whenever he mentioned the subject in his letters, he was always referring to the Castle Leslie entertainments. 'My present sideline,' he informed his mother,

> is to arrange some sort of production for next time we go there. I am trying to make arrangements for several of the family to take part in it. Then we could make quite a good job of it. Two reading the parts, two working figures and one working lights, gramophone, sound effects, etc. So don't worry about afterwards. It is only the model theatre interests me.

Desmond as a teenager just before the outbreak of the Second World War with pony Ralteen.

Writing, acting, playing music: it seemed as though Desmond was capable of doing anything he wanted. 'I was given too many talents,' he ruminated in 1981, 'and eventually I had to bury some of them.' But that was in the future. As a teenager he had the energy and enthusiasm to pursue all his diverse interests and still have time for study during school term and an active social life over the holidays.

Despite Partition, the Leslies continued to see friends on the other side of the border. An undated letter written by Desmond to his mother describes a visit he made to Florence Court in County Fermanagh, a house now owned by the National Trust but then still home to the Earl and Countess of Enniskillen. 'I thought I'd let you know that I've arrived and am having a heavenly time,' he told Marjorie. 'Went to Baron's Court yesterday where they are excavating a crannagh. This house is the most lovely old building with a huge rambling basement … I am in a haunted room which refuses to function. Apparently one is meant to go mad, but such could never happen to a genuine Leslie. We could only become madder!'

Throughout these years, Marjorie continued to be an indefatigable traveller, often taking Anita with her until in 1937 the latter married Russian officer Paul Rodzianko (whose uncle was head of the pre-Revolutionary Duma). By then Desmond was old enough to join his mother, as he did on a trip to Portugal the following New Year. He and Marjorie stayed in Lisbon with the American ambassador Herbert Pell and enjoyed a hectic social life.

'Today the diplomatic corps (us included) went on a picnic which may cause a world war,' he wrote to his brother Jack,

> It was icy cold and too funny for words! Ambassadorial limousines filled with gorging diplomats (and us!) trying to eat and keep warm. Cakes and wine glasses parked on the roof, and others diving headfirst into baskets for coffee. I took some amusing photos, of a type that would cause a breaking off of diplomatic relations were they ever shown.

He devoted an afternoon to walking around the slums of Lisbon, 'which are very poor indeed', although 'the people are very nice and courteous and don't gape at you like a half-witted fish out of water like the French do. They are not grabbing and always give you the right change.'

The following year, 1939, Desmond took his final exams and left Ampleforth. He had grown tall, six foot four inches, and was extremely handsome – like a reincarnation of Byron, says his second wife Helen. Attractive to women, he had fallen in love some years before with a beautiful cousin, Clarissa Churchill, whose father was Winston Churchill's younger brother Jack. She had come to stay at Castle Leslie with her mother and been taken out riding by the enamoured Desmond. Unfortunately, he made the mistake of lending her his own frisky mare, which promptly bolted; rushing through trees, Clarissa Churchill was hit by a branch and thrown concussed to the ground. It was the end of Desmond's earliest efforts at courtship – he grew much better with practice – and in 1952 Clarissa Churchill married Anthony Eden, soon afterwards appointed as British prime minister.

Meanwhile, during the summer of 1939, a decision had to be made about what eighteen-year-old Desmond should do now that he had left school. This matter became more critical after Britain declared war against Germany in August. Jack was already an officer in the Irish Guards and Anita would eventually sign up for war work, but both of them were considerably older than Desmond. When war was declared, he was at Castle Leslie with his father. 'I remember getting off my horse and going through the gate by the water tower and a man there said, "The war's on".' Later that evening, he sat in his grandmother Leonie's room listening to a radio broadcast of Neville Chamberlain, the British prime minister, officially declaring hostilities against Germany, 'and granny said, "Don't worry, we shall win. We always do."'

Jack (left) and Desmond on the terrace of Castle Leslie shortly before the Second World War.

It was agreed between Desmond and his father that he should remain in Ireland, studying at Trinity College, Dublin. Ostensibly he went there in the autumn to read philosophy; his son Mark thinks this subject was chosen 'because he thought it would involve sitting under a tree with a guru'. Later he would claim to have attended only two lectures in the course of a year, preferring to spend most of his time building a four-poster bed in his college rooms, where he also installed two manual organs, rented for five shillings a week, 'to the despair of my very serious, hard-swotting neighbours who actually went to college to study'. At the same time he enrolled for tuition at the Royal Irish Academy of Music where 'once again I felt the constraint of orthodox harmony like a jacket that didn't fit. I could hear wondrous sounds, but how to express them? How splendid it would be, I thought, if someone could "think these sounds into reality by some device". The invention of the tape recorder produced the device I was seeking.'

Because Ireland was officially neutral, it suffered few of the privations being experienced across the Irish Sea. There were no blackouts and plenty of nightlife for a young man enjoying independence after many years at an all-male boarding school. Anita remembered that on the occasions when Desmond did come to London during the first year of war, 'he only wanted a telephone on which to ring girls'. However, in the spring of 1940 he discovered that he would have to sit an exam at Trinity College and show evidence of academic application over the previous months. Already rather bored of undergraduate life in Dublin, he began to look for a way out. A college friend had gone to Belfast and joined the Royal Air Force. Desmond decided to do likewise.

T
H
R
E
E

WHEN STILL A SCHOOLBOY at Ampleforth, Desmond had written to his mother:

> It is too maddening to see that we would go to war if Hitler invaded Czechoslovakia, which is a nasty little half-Red country. Personally I don't care a damn about it or any other nation of that type, and to think that we would be willing to sacrifice millions of lives and the safety of our nation on their account is absurd.

But circumstances and attitudes change. By the time he signed up to join the RAF, Desmond's brother Jack was already a German prisoner of war and would remain as such for the next five years. Meanwhile his sister Anita had joined the women's Mechanised Transport Corps and his father Shane was enrolled in the Home Guard in London. Marjorie had returned to Castle Leslie where she would remain for the duration of the war, during which time both her elderly parents-in-law died, Leonie in August 1943 and Papa Jack just five months later.

Given the involvement of his family in the war effort, it is not hard to understand why Desmond, even allowing for his desire to escape academic life at Trinity College, would also want to participate. Much of what he experienced over the next three years later served as copy for his first novel *Careless Lives*, whose hero Julien Rayburn is obviously modelled on the author. Its title taken from the well-known wartime slogan 'Careless Talk Costs Lives', one of the book's earliest chapters describes Julien being summoned from London to an RAF base in Devon where he gets to meet his fellow recruits and 'for the first time realized he was going to live with men from every trade, every creed, every class … They were all in the job together, and it seemed a great chance of making friends and learning things he would never have learned during his four years' cricket-playing' at his privileged public school. During this early stage in the RAF, mornings were passed in drill and 'square bashing' while the afternoons were taken up with lectures that left many of the participants feeling they were back at school: 'They dropped books, threw chalk, made inky paper darts, ragged the lecturers and were kept in if they got bad marks. "After all," said Julien, "shooting up Huns in a Spitfire is only a glorification of the inky dart phase".'

Desmond also told his son Mark of an occasion when he and a large number of other new recruits were ordered to attend a lecture at the Odeon cinema in London's Leicester Square. The instructor failed to appear and the troops threatened to grow restive but then Desmond discovered how to operate the premises' Wurlitzer organ; it duly rose at the front of the auditorium and he entertained his captive audience with a selection of popular tunes.

Eventually desk-bound theory had to give way to practical training and this, Desmond learnt, was to take place in the United

States. Although both his mother and grandmother were American, he had never before visited the country and his wonder at what he found there is expressed both in an airbase newsletter he edited in June 1942 and within the pages of *Careless Lives*. The former explains how he and the other trainee pilots travelled across the Atlantic in mid-winter 1940 in a converted meat transporter, sleeping in hammocks slung from hooks that until then had carried carcasses. Hammocks, he wrote, did not make comfortable beds. 'They are statically and dynamically unstable and possess alarming stalling characteristics and are apt to snap-roll you onto the floor, just as you, poor sucker, imagine you have got them properly trimmed for the night.' The conditions on board were harsh and the weather poor. 'In spite of much food on board, there was little digested. One way or another, the trip could be described as rough.'

Eventually the ship docked on the Canadian coast and the entire troupe transferred on to a train that travelled, via brief stops in Boston, New York and Washington, to Florida where 'it finally came to rest in the middle of the Everglades at a place called Clewiston. The camp in those days consisted of two things: mud and buildings, the latter poking their way up like little white mushrooms, slightly bewildered at the indescribable mess.' At this stage the United States was not yet officially at war and could not therefore be seen overtly to support the British effort. Desmond and his fellow British recruits, although training under the auspices of the US Air Corps, were accordingly obliged to wear civilian clothes rather than their RAF uniforms, and to give the impression of blending in with the locals. This did little to encourage discipline, especially since the caps of the American commanding officers were remarkably similar to those worn by local taxi drivers; the young British trainees were inclined to greet their superiors with the cry of 'Taxi!' As a result, on at least one occasion Desmond was sentenced, for insubordination, to an hour's dummy flying; this involved his dashing up and down a hot runway dressed in full flying paraphernalia while calling out manoeuvres to the control tower. One of his colleagues, when given the same punishment, decided to follow the Rule Book's observation that all manoeuvres were permissible: he declared himself obliged to make a forced landing; pulled his parachute; jumped into the fire pool; and inflated a rubber dinghy while firing his pistol to attract the attention of passing aircraft.

Initial training took place in mock cockpits on the ground before the would-be pilots were taken up for their first flight. 'Fifteen minutes was all it lasted,' wrote Desmond, 'and we came down exhausted. That first turn at two hundred feet seemed to us the height of all that is daring and skilful.' Sometime later came the day when they were, at last, permitted to fly unaccompanied by an instructor: 'No more nattering down the speaking-tube. No more being cursed for every small fault. You know you can do it … because you've done it many times with him. Now you have nothing to distract you, and simply do it on your own.'

Desmond in his plane during the Second World War.

Desmond's commanding officer was Nelson Jay, ten years his senior and with a background in smuggling and flying for the Continental Oil Company during the 1930s. He and Desmond quickly bonded and for a variety of reasons would remain in contact until the older man's death in 1993. In *Careless Lives* he is named Hank Renzel, 'a large, smiling native of Florida who had three thousand flying hours to his credit … He was intrigued and amused at Julien's Mayfair brogue, and asked him whether he took his top hat off to go to bed. Julien replied by offering him some gum, and the two became fast friends.'

Between training, there were opportunities to enjoy Palm Beach, where at the Everglades Club 'we would dance out under the stars, 'neath fifty-foot palms softly lit while the moon cascaded over Lake Worth in showers of molten gold', or the trainees could relax at the Bath and Tennis Club, 'a Spanish palace set down by the sea, well upholstered in beautiful women, vast lunches, blue pools and ultra exclusive sand'. Sometimes it was possible to venture further afield to New Orleans or New York. Desmond recalled one ten-day leave that ended on a Sunday night when 'a series of living wrecks stumbled into camp, utterly dissipated and worn out. Consequently, utterly happy.' Compared to war-ravaged England where food was rationed, at the Florida camp 'the canteen was and is an endless source of attraction. There we could get all the things we couldn't get at home.' In fact, as *Careless Lives* makes plain, everything about the United States was an endless source of attraction for Desmond, not least the women he met during his time there. In the novel Julien attends a party in Palm Beach where he encounters the host's daughter Carole. At first sight of her, he 'staggered, closed his eyes and opened them again, but the vision was still there, smiling at him provocatively. The long, black hair was very black, and the emphatic young body seemed almost to be bursting from the one white close-fitting garment.' Given Desmond's subsequent record

Desmond and Anne Reinecke on top of Empire State Building during the Second World War.

with women, it seems fair to assume there was more than one model for the character of Carole who soon introduces to his hero such pleasures as 'American dancing', which 'was a little unnerving, and bad for anyone with a weak heart'.

Equally amazing, in his young eyes, were American homes and nightclubs and cars and motorways and skyscrapers.

Circumstances changed somewhat after 7 December 1941 when the Japanese air force bombed Pearl Harbour, the American naval base in Hawaii, and the United States officially entered the war. To begin with, the RAF trainees were now required to wear their uniforms but this was not a problem; doing so, they found, led to their being hailed as heroes and showered with praise whenever they left camp. Strolling along the Miami seafront in his uniform, Desmond found himself stopped by two strangers who insisted on giving him a free manicure, haircut and shave in their adjacent premises. Although he found it a little strange that these services were provided while he lay flat on a leather-covered bench, he was happy to take advantage of the offer. Only on leaving did he look at the sign outside the building and realize his benefactors had been morticians working for an undertaker.

Flight training eventually came to an end and despite Florida's delights the qualified British pilots were expected to return home. 'We have learned many things,' wrote Desmond in the June 1942 newsletter, 'not the least of which is Southern Hospitality. We've certainly had a time, and America, we thank you for it … One day we will come to Florida again, and see the friends we have made, and the great hearted people who made their homes our homes on this side of the water.'

Back in England, Flight Sergeant Desmond Leslie now began flying Spitfires. After the war ended he would declare himself responsible for destroying a large number of aircraft, before confessing that he had been flying most of them at the time of their annihilation. He certainly seems to have had an exceptional ability for getting himself into – and out of – trouble while on duty. Once, for example, an approaching enemy plane managed to rip off the rudder of Desmond's Spitfire and leave him trapped in the cockpit; he was forced to make an emergency landing on a nearby bomber-base runway, escaping from his machine only just before it blew up. Conveniently a family friend, 'Ginger' Boyle – otherwise Admiral of the Fleet William Henry Dudley Boyle, 12th Earl of Cork and Orrery – was visiting the base at the time and immediately offered Desmond a lift back to camp in his car.

He also inadvertently managed to set the RAF record for aerial gunnery. All pilots were tested for their skill in this area by firing while

Desmond posing in profile as a pilot during the Second World War.

in flight at a windsock – known as a drogue – attached to the rear of another plane. At the time Desmond was tested he was posted to an airbase near Prestwick in Scotland. Unfortunately, he remembered, on the day in question, 'I had a rather big boil on my arse.' The boil caused him to flinch in pain and grip the trigger at precisely the moment he had to fire at the windsock; emptying almost his entire magazine he managed to send the majority of his bullets directly into their intended target. Owing to the boil, 'I was told to go on sick leave afterwards, so that one burst on target stood as my average. Of course, I couldn't possibly have done it if I'd intended to. Nobody could.'

Given to causing mischief, sometimes he was unable to escape reprimand from his commanding officer, such as the day he tried sky-writing with a vapour trail from his Spitfire. He had got as far as spelling out F, U and C when an oil leak forced him to abandon the effort and return to base. Unfortunately the first faint trail of a K had been traced in the same black smoke coming from the grounded Spitfire, thereby identifying Desmond as the culprit. Similarly, when posted to a base in the west of England, he and his fellow pilots found a bridge over the river Severn, the span of which was only a few feet wider than that of their plane wings. They took to flying regularly under the bridge as a dare until a local publican complained of the noise, after which the site was officially placed out of bounds to RAF aircraft. Determined to disobey this regulation, a group of pilots chose to attempt the manoeuvre at dusk when their planes would be least identifiable to the pub owner. Desmond was the last under the bridge but, having successfully come through, he clipped the pub's hanging sign and sent it flying; his Spitfire was subsequently recognized as responsible thanks to a dent and scratched paintwork. He was charged with 'Handling His Majesty's aircraft in a manner prejudicial to good order'.

Though relatively well-paid, he still looked for ways to save money. Agnes Bernelle recalled that not long after meeting Desmond, she travelled with him by train. When the two of them reached their destination, he handed the ticket-collector a piece of paper and then told Agnes to run. Later he told her, 'I gave him my laundry list. I always travel on my laundry list.' A surviving letter he wrote to his commanding officer, dated 28 April 1943, deals with the question of a missing train ticket, Desmond insisting that on a journey he made between Oxford and Paddington Station two weeks earlier his ticket had been 'lost somewhere between the barrier at Oxford and the Gentlemen's toilet at Reading'. He argued that access even to the station platform would not have been possible without a ticket since this was 'guarded by a most formidable barrier, which the Great Western Railway has equipped with beings of impressive stature, and hawk-eyed vigilance having in their right hands the callipers of righteousness, and wearing on their foreheads the mystic word "Inspector"; no doubt as a deterrent to impoverished airmen'.

Desmond was inclined to give the impression that his time in the RAF had consisted of little other than a sequence of high-spirited larks. Being a Flight Sergeant pilot, he told writer Stan Gebler Davies in the early 1980s, was wonderful because he had no mess bills to pay:

> It was the only time in my life I've ever been in the black. You were given twenty-seven shillings and six pence a week and half a crown danger money. Beer was sixpence a pint, the movies were nine pence and the girls were free. I kept a suite with a friend at Grosvenor House. It was only two pounds a night if you were in uniform, but you had to have a suite because if you only had a room you couldn't have a girl in it or the house dick would get you.

Careless Lives captures this youthful insouciance, the novel opening with Julien Rayburn and his friends drinking in the suite of a 'luxurious Mayfair hotel' before the whole group moves on to a basement nightclub in Berkeley Street where, despite enemy bombs dropping over London, 'oysters, caviar and inferior champagne flowed. Pay-rolls evaporated, and everyone was happy, or pretended to be.' It was, perhaps, easier for members of the RAF to convey an impression of indifference to danger than for their equivalents in the army or navy; cocooned within their planes, they usually had to think only of their own welfare. Though death was a constant threat, it also remained something of an abstract concept, since they rarely saw any of their fellow pilots die. And if someone was lost on a mission, it was always possible to believe he had successfully bailed out or been captured by the enemy.

Desmond was in a particularly privileged position, given that the prime minister, Churchill, was his first cousin once-removed. He took advantage of this relationship to return to Ireland for the funeral of his grandmother Leonie Leslie in August 1943, informing his superiors that Churchill would want him to be present. An RAF bomber flown by two senior officers was requisitioned to fly Desmond across the Irish Sea and it circled over Castle Leslie before dropping a note requesting a car to be sent across the border; he arrived at the family home just as the funeral cortège was about to leave. On another occasion Desmond was invited by Churchill to have dinner and stay overnight at Chequers, the prime minister's official country residence in Buckinghamshire. Here he found himself keeping company with senior members of the Allied Forces while news came through of a large-scale bombing offensive against Germany. Desmond recalled Churchill's tears of despair as he calculated the loss of life among British crews who had failed to return from the mission.

This spectacle increased Desmond's already growing disillusion with his life in the RAF. By 1943 the German air force had been gravely weakened and Spitfires were no longer as much in demand for direct combat. Instead, their pilots were increasingly used as escorts on the strategic area bombing missions promoted by Air Marshall Sir Arthur 'Bomber' Harris. This kind of activity was not to Desmond's taste and it is interesting to speculate what he might have done had his health not forced his early retirement from the RAF. Late in 1943 he returned from a flight to the base in Taunton where he was then based and, on stepping out of the cockpit, fainted on the tarmac. Though planes at that period were capable of climbing up to 30,000 feet, their interiors were not yet pressurized. A medical check revealed Desmond had a damaged heart, which could lead to his passing out while on duty were he to continue flying; this would have meant the loss of both pilot and aircraft.

In 1944 he was invalided out of the RAF on a pension of seven shillings and six pence a week. For the rest of the war, he worked in London for the Office of War Information established by the American government, editing radio news bulletins and propaganda broadcasts. He also used the time to write *Careless Lives*, which was based on his own wartime experiences and appeared before the year ended 'in complete conformity with the War Economy Agreement'. Dedicated to 'My brother John, a Prisoner of War', the novel became a bestseller. 'Mainly owing to the lack of material,' said Desmond self-deprecatingly.

F
O
U
R

BY THE TIME he was discharged from the RAF, Desmond had fallen in love with the woman who would become his first wife. Agnes Bernelle – known as Agi to her family and friends – had been born in Berlin in 1923, the daughter of a successful Hungarian theatre impresario, Rudolf Bernauer, who also wrote cabaret lyrics. Bernauer was Jewish and with the rise of the Nazi party in Germany he lost his livelihood and property, and was forced to flee to England where he was joined in 1936 by his daughter and later by his wife. Settling in London, he wrote and directed low-budget films while Agnes finished her schooling. Her ambition to be an actress received a setback with the outbreak of war in 1939 when the Bernauers, who held Hungarian passports, were classified as enemy aliens. However, she soon began to perform with the Freier Deutscher Kulturbund, or Free German League of Culture, and to appear with a number of touring production companies. After the United States joined the war, she was recruited by the Office of Strategic Service and started presenting radio broadcasts to Germany, called *Vicky with the Three Kisses*, on behalf of the Allies. In her memoir, *The Fun Palace*, Agnes tells of how one German submarine commander was persuaded to surface and surrender off the coast of Scotland after hearing Vicky congratulate him on air on the birth of a son. 'And I haven't been home for more than two years,' he indignantly declared.

Agnes met Desmond at a party in London in 1943, one of those hedonistic occasions he describes in *Careless Lives* where 'a group of decorative young people' were determined to enjoy themselves no matter what disaster might befall them the following day. The party took place in the Mayfair home of Lady Winifride Elwes, widow of the English tenor Gervase Elwes and mother of portraitist Simon Elwes. Agnes, who was unused to being invited to such smart events, had turned up hopelessly overdressed in her mother's black evening dress and her aunt's diamonds. Nevertheless, she made enough of an impression on Desmond to end the night being kissed by him in the back of a taxi. 'For the next week,' she wrote in *The Fun Palace*, 'we spent every possible moment together to make the best of his leave,' Desmond then still being in the RAF. Soon they were lovers, Agnes having been seduced during a night in a hotel in Henley-on-Thames, and not long afterwards Desmond proposed marriage.

News of his intentions met with a mixed response from other members of the Leslie family. Jack was still a prisoner of war and Anita by this time was acting as an ambulance driver in the Middle East; both were therefore largely incommunicado. Shane, based in London, met Agnes and gave his approval. On the other hand Marjorie, from the fastness of Castle Leslie, did not. Her attitude was undoubtedly coloured by the reports of Desmond's fiancée she received from her brother-in-law Seymour. Apparently he 'did not approve of

Publicity shot of Agnes, mid-1950s.

Desmond's liaison with a penniless refugee who, horror upon horror, was on the stage'. Desmond's second novel, *Pardon My Return*, published in 1946, contains a fictional portrait of the meddling Seymour Leslie – here called Uncle Zombey – sending similarly highly charged reports back home of his nephew's behaviour in London. Soon after meeting the book's hero Rory with an 'unsuitable' young woman, Zombey writes a long letter, 'effulgent, authoritative, advisory', back to Cruiskeen where the Headstone family react with horror to what he tells them. So too did Marjorie Leslie on hearing from Seymour of Desmond and Agnes's engagement: she took to her bed declaring that her younger son had promised not to become engaged without speaking to his mother first. A complete collapse followed and she was soon installed in a comfortable Dublin nursing home.

Cover of Desmond's 1946 novel, Pardon My Return.

'I don't know where she gets the idea that I made any solemn promise,' Desmond wrote to his father. 'I promised not to marry for the time being, but said nothing about being engaged. I would have got engaged months ago but postponed it in the hope she would get well enough to come here.' In an oblique reference to his uncle Seymour he added, 'What I shall not forgive for a long time are the people who have tried to poison her mind against Agnes … people who do not know and don't trouble to find out.' Desmond asked his father to intervene with Marjorie on the couple's behalf.

> Perhaps when she is in the mood, you can pluck up enough courage to remove some of her misconceptions about her future daughter-in-law. She will not listen to me and for her own good I never mention the subject now. You have seen Agnes enough by now to recognize that she is one of the few lovely girls who are also good and true and have all the rare qualities so admirable in women but unfortunately so hard to find nowadays.

But he did have some allies in Ireland, among them a former girlfriend called JoJo O'Reilly. Born in Burma and christened Helen Lentaigne, she had been raised in Ireland before moving to London and joining the Women's Auxiliary Air Force, which is presumably how she met Desmond. In 1944 she had a baby (the first of twelve) who would eventually become the writer Victor O'Reilly, his surname taken from JoJo's husband Terence O'Reilly (the first of three), whom she married soon after the birth. Following her death in 2001, Victor O'Reilly described his mother as 'charismatic, creative and inspirational', adding that throughout her life 'she did what she wanted when she wanted and to hell with convention and political correctness'. Her character comes through in a letter she wrote to Desmond during the time he was trying to persuade his mother that Agnes Bernelle would be a suitable wife. Then living at Newtown House, Termonfeckin, County Louth (now called An Grianán and serving as headquarters for the Irish Countrywomen's

Association), JoJo addressed Desmond as 'Mon cher petit spiced and scented consort,' before going on to say:

> Agnes does sound a wow (what a nauseating expression). I am determined to be her first girlfriend in Ireland for two very good reasons. (1) It will help my prestige and (2) The contrast between us will show her to her best advantage even in the eyes of the two test tubes from which you found life. They will realize what a terrible creature you might have fallen for had you been less discriminating, and will receive Agnes with open arms in gratitude that I was no more than one of your over-perfumed, betrousered, cheap Northern concubines.

Nonetheless, Marjorie continued to resist the notion of Desmond and Agnes being married. It didn't help that *Tatler* published a photograph of the pair together, a picture that, Desmond declared, made 'Agnes look like a puffy negress with spots. I look like a dying cow with jaundice.' In the end it was agreed that he should go to Ireland and placate Marjorie, by now back at Castle Leslie. Immediately she did her best to detain him with tasks about the estate for long enough to make his engagement become a distant memory. 'He sent me amusing letters almost daily,' Agnes recalled, 'but several months went by and he did not return … It was apparent that his mother was deliberately keeping him from me with many tasks and diversions, and he did not seem to mind.' In *Pardon My Return* Rory Headstone is likewise discouraged by his family from returning to London and his fiancée Thistle Conlon who, after receiving yet another letter from distant Ireland, asks herself: 'Did he calmly imagine that she would forever patiently await his return? Let him get on with his dishonest pigs and disorderly hens if they were more important than herself … Let him sit there happily among his ancestral cowpats.'

Agnes did her best to be patient and to let Desmond know she was devoting as much time to his career as her own. 'Dearest,' she wrote, 'I am trying to sell *Careless Lives* to a film firm. When do you think one can lay hands on a copy? I've sent them the little write-up and a friend is doing her best to interest the producer in it.' Meanwhile, she was being entertained in London by Desmond's naughty godfather, Evan Morgan, who 'was terribly sweet and wrote a smashing introduction to Noel Coward telling him that he will find me "remarkably charming, intelligent and interesting". I shall have to attach a little note when I send it to him warning him against any illusions about me as, in simple fact, I am an actress!' But after waiting several months, Agnes eventually decided to force the issue by writing to Desmond with the news that she was breaking off their engagement. He immediately responded by asking her to come to Ireland.

Having secured permission to leave wartime Britain, she made the journey and was met by Desmond in Dublin. After a few days in the city, the couple travelled to Castle Leslie where Agnes was finally introduced to Marjorie, an occasion which should have been fraught with drama but actually proved to be a great success, since the two women instantly took to one another. 'Can't imagine what that naughty Uncle Seymour thought he was doing when he wrote to me from London,' said Marjorie. 'You do not look a bit like the person he has been describing.' Indeed, she so liked Agnes that the young couple were offered the use of Marjorie's London residence after their wedding. In 1939, before moving to Castle Leslie, she had given up her lease on the house in Westbourne Terrace and taken a large, fifth-floor flat in South Lodge, St John's Wood.

Back in England, Desmond wrote to his father, 'We had a perfect visit to Glaslough. Agnes and Ma hit it off from the start, and the people of the place fell in love with her. We only had four days but they were the most perfect four days. No doubt Ma has written you most of the details.' One detail Marjorie may not have written about, presumably because she was not a witness to it, was later described by Agnes in *The Fun Palace*: Desmond came to her room late at night after dinner and insisted she follow him for a nude frolic in the garden. Though terrified they would be seen by her future mother-in-law, Agnes 'decided to risk it and there we were, like two fairy children, our bodies white in the moonlight, holding hands and dancing round the tree'.

Wedding photo of Desmond and Agnes, 1945.

Desmond and Agnes were married on 18 August 1945, just days after the official Allied victory celebrations had taken place in London; on that occasion, the two of them had cycled to 10 Downing Street to deliver a bottle of wine to Desmond's cousin, Winston Churchill. The wedding ceremony was held at St James's Church, Spanish Place, with both Marjorie and Shane present; the latter wore his saffron kilt because, as Desmond wrote in a letter beforehand, 'It would be original and picturesque and in keeping with family tradition.' Witnesses included Desmond's godfather Evan Morgan, Lord Tredegar and also Beatrice Violet, Lady Leconfield.

Desmond's brother Jack, now finally released from prison camp, was best man, while a couple of Agnes's friends from her time at school in England acted as bridesmaids. She wore a dress of white satin brocade, old material Desmond had found in a chest at Castle Leslie, and a veil lent to her by Marjorie. A friend had filmed the VE Day celebrations and now used his camera to record the wedding, afterwards giving the entire spool to the couple as a present. Later Desmond spliced shots of the two events together and when his sons Sean and Mark were young, they were convinced that the cheering and singing crowds lining London's streets had gathered for the sole purpose of witnessing their parents' marriage. In fact, the occasion was marked by a rather smaller number of people; after the church ceremony some forty family members and friends were invited back to South Lodge in St John's Wood for champagne and a fork lunch. Numbers were limited because wartime rationing still prevailed and in any case, Desmond warned his sociable father, should any more guests be asked, 'the flat will burst and the bride's father will be broke'. The couple spent their wedding night at the Berkeley Hotel and then returned to South Lodge. It would be their home until they moved to Ireland in 1963.

With peace declared and his job at the Office of War Information therefore finished, Desmond had to think about earning a living. Although he received an allowance from his mother, and also some money from a trust established by his aunt Anne Bourke Cockran, who died in 1945, this was not enough to meet his and Agnes's needs, especially after the arrival of their first child Sean, born in June 1947. Since the death of his grandfather, Castle Leslie officially belonged to his older brother Jack who now lived there with their mother Marjorie while Shane continued to be based primarily in London. Back from her own wartime adventures, in 1949 Anita would marry her second husband Commander Bill King and with him settle at Oranmore Castle, County Galway.

Agnes and Desmond at Sean's christening in 1947. Agnes's mother Emy Bernauer is behind Agnes to the left. Desmond's father Shane Leslie is above and directly behind Evan Morgan, Viscount Tredegar, on Desmond's left.

With one novel already published, Desmond decided to become a writer. 'I'm very busy every moment of the day,' he had told his father just before the wedding when he was working 'on another book and film stories. I lunch a lot and make useful contacts. It is fun being kept busy.' He also did his best to help promote Agnes's acting career, such as the time she was up for the part of an Egyptian handmaiden in the lavish film adaptation of George Bernard Shaw's *Caesar and Cleopatra* with Claude Rains and Vivien Leigh in the title roles. Desmond accompanied Agnes to the audition and then slipped away, suddenly reappearing in a seat beside director Gabriel Pascal just as Agnes appeared, when he loudly declaimed his preference for 'That one. The curvy one with the squashy lips!' Though Agnes did get the part, ill health meant she was unavailable for filming. Over the next decade, she worked intermittently while bringing up two children and trying to keep her husband under control, the latter task frequently more challenging than the former.

Desmond's second novel, *Pardon My Return*, was published in 1946 and while large sections of the book are set on a decaying Irish country estate called Cruiskeen Castle that is not unlike Castle Leslie, other parts of it concern the protagonist's efforts to become involved in the British film industry. Rory Headstone moves to London in search of a job as a scriptwriter at Hollocast Productions Ltd and later sets up his own, spectacularly unsuccessful, production company, its failure caused in part by Rory's chronic lack of good time-keeping, something that would also bedevil Desmond throughout his adult life. 'Why has the industry never turned out a picture that can rank as art?' Rory rhetorically asks, before arguing that the explanation lay in the film world being run 'as a business concern to a timetable. When I make a film, there will be no clocks allowed in the studio. The director will only stop work when he and the artists feel their inspiration is on the ebb. It will be a picture made of soul rather than celluloid.' To which his business partner dryly responds, 'You will doubtless come up against the unions who have rather pronounced views on technicians' working hours.' Desmond's business skills were never going to be very strong. Later he would write that he gave up trying to make films because 'there are easier ways of not earning money'.

But in the second half of the 1940s his enthusiasm for film had not yet been blunted. One of his early scripts, called *Smuggler's Paradise*, bears a lot of similarities to *Pardon My Return*, being once more set in the fictional Cruiskeen Castle and concerning the efforts of the self-same Rory Headstone to earn an income and to marry a girl who meets with disapproval from the rest of his family. As the title makes clear, the plot also involves cross-border smuggling plus an attempt to set up an independent republic, making *Smuggler's Paradise* read like a strange amalgamation between *The Quiet Man*, *Whisky Galore* and *Passport to Pimlico*. Not surprisingly, it was never made into a film. Undeterred, in 1947 Desmond formed a production company, Leinster Films, and then wrote and co-directed his first feature *Stranger at My Door*.

Publicity for Desmond's 1950 film, Stranger at My Door.

A crime thriller, the story tells of a young Dublin man's attempts to buy his girlfriend various expensive presents beyond his means, eventually resorting to burglary because he cannot afford to pay for them; later he discovers she has been using the money he brought her to pay off an extortionist. Partly filmed at Castle Leslie, it featured Agnes in a lead role alongside Valentine Dyall and Joseph O'Connor and was made on money raised from various sources, including a number of Marjorie Leslie's richer friends. It seems unlikely they recouped their investment because the film made little impact on its initial release in 1950 and is now entirely forgotten. Nevertheless at that stage Desmond considered this just the beginning of his career in cinema and around the time *Stranger at My Door* was released, he wrote in a feature for *Picture Post* that 'I have found at Glaslough ideal conditions for making feature films at a quarter of the cost required in a studio, and we shall start the first this summer.'

It didn't happen, perhaps because even at a quarter of the studio costs, Desmond still had trouble raising the necessary cash. Agnes's memoir is full of tales of the young couple's chronic lack of money; once she found her husband disconsolately sitting in the lobby of Dublin's Shelbourne Hotel after his suitcase had been impounded because he was unable to pay the bill. Another time, in order to cover the cost of a stay in Amsterdam, she had to sell most of her clothes to the hotel barman. Without the price of tickets to the annual Film Ball held at London's Royal Albert Hall, Desmond and Agnes dressed up – he in his brother Jack's dinner jacket, she in her mother's fur stole – hired a car to bring them from the back of the building to the main entrance and then swept inside with such confidence that nobody thought to question whether or not they should be there. There were various schemes intended to make them rich quickly, such as advertising copies of the Bible as the 'scandalous book no one can afford to miss' or offering for sale hand-made leprechauns Desmond had imported from Ireland, but none of these came to anything. Shortage of money would be one of his most pressing problems for the next half-century.

F I V E

In THE LATE 1940s as a way of increasing his income Desmond took up journalism for which he had a natural bent. It wasn't long before he was regularly contributing to a number of magazines including *Picture Post* and *Illustrated*. The latter, for example, carried his amusing photo-essay on cross-border smuggling between the Republic and Northern Ireland in which 'secret ways of running contraband are re-enacted for *Illustrated*'. Nor was he shy about taking advantage of contacts, such as when in September 1950 he wrote a story for *Picture Post* about his distant relative the Duke of Marlborough opening Blenheim Palace to the general public or, just three months later, a charming feature on the Christmas show staged by pupils at his old prep school Ladycross where 'the chorus sit around, swinging their nimble legs, hoping they'll get a line or two during rehearsals and wondering what's for tea'. And, of

Vol. 47 No. 2

PICTURE POST

8 April, 1950

The Family Coach That is Used When Petrol is Short

Major John Madden and his estate workers trundle out the Waterloo carriage, of the type sat in by Wellington. It's the kind of thing you'll find in the coach-house on most Irish estates. It enlivens local funerals. It also smartens up weddings and other state occasions.

IRELAND'S CASTLES

GRANDEUR IN DECLINE

Photographed by HAYWOOD MAGEE

THE Harp that once through Tara's halls, etc.," and all the other songs, ballads and dirges extolling the glory of that great pre-Christian neighbours on the head, not for weaving into regal residences. More likely Tara and Emmania were made of wood, were draughty, were dank, were of

Article written by Desmond in Picture Post, 8 April 1950.

course, he wrote about Ireland, specifically the milieu with which he was familiar. In August 1950, *Picture Post* carried a spread by Desmond on the Dublin Horse Show where, he informed readers, 'the horse, the Supreme Quadruped, is the Most Important Creature, always has been, always will be. Here, as a reward for his self-sacrifice, ceaseless devotion and unflagging services rendered during the preceding year, Man is allowed to tag along too in the capacity of stooge, valet-de-chambre, coiffeur, masseur, bottle-washer and passionate fan to Horse.'

The Irish country house was another subject with which Desmond had an especial affinity, and he wrote on it for both *Picture Post* and *Vogue*, becoming extravagantly lyrical as he described the 'wild beauty in Irish demesnes, absent in English estates. The trees are enormous, 120 feet being average for conifers; the woods tangled and impenetrable; gigantic Arthur Rackham roots straddle quivering bog, and in the dark lakes huge old fish lie or else bask in the amber pools where branches sweep down to kiss the water.' Given his own later experience of struggling to hang on to Castle Leslie, it is interesting to read Desmond in *Vogue's* July 1951 edition magisterially commenting that 'So far the Irish country house seems happily to have evaded the doom of the English, which now seems inevitably destined to end up as an Egg Inspectorate or Regional Sewage Board. The creak of the tumbril sounds further off in Ireland – perhaps another couple of generations. The roof is still on, the butler still loyal and the crests on the entrance gates show no signs of rust.' Not much more than a decade later, Desmond must have rued ever writing those words.

But in the early 1950s, he was still a young man with the prospect of almost anything being possible, married to a beautiful actress and, despite the relative shortage of money, enjoying an extremely busy social life in both London and Ireland. When visiting Castle Leslie, Agnes remembered, she and Desmond would travel to stay in other houses where 'you still had your suitcase unpacked and packed again by your hostess's lady's maid, and had your bath run for you while you were changing for dinner'. Though at times he appeared to rebel against his upbringing, Desmond was in many ways a conservative and a product of his family background. 'Heredity and conviction made him a confirmed Tory,' proclaims the author's blurb on the reverse of his third novel, *Angels Weep*, which was published in 1948. With a sombre tone quite different from the levity of its two predecessors, this is a dystopian vision of the near future very similar in spirit to

Agnes posing by the pool in the 1950s.

George Orwell's *1984*, which appeared just a year later. Indeed, the hero of *Angels Weep*, John Brown, shares many characteristics with Orwell's Winston Smith: both characters work for a totalitarian state in mundane jobs that offer little satisfaction; both live in wretched, government-owned accommodation; both understand they must keep their feelings concealed at all times; and both eventually face execution as the result of a clandestine affair. *Angels Weep* is by no means as fine a work of fiction as *1984*; it is clumsier in concept and execution, but it displays the post-war era's widespread fear of government despotism as exemplified by Stalinist Russia. 'All the isms, socialism, fascism, communism are all, in their muddled angry way, trying to say the same thing,' says Anna Smith, the girl with whom John Brown falls in love.

Desmond and Agnes with Sean feeding birds, c.1952–3.

A set of idealists destroy a set of tyrants only to be destroyed by their own corruption. Then a few years later you need another set of idealists to liberate the people, with bigger and better massacres and more comprehensive purges. And so it goes on with the final state no better than the first, and no one any happier.

What *Angels Weep* does offer is an insight into the author's intense interest in, and knowledge of, music. John Brown wants to be a composer, but is unable to receive the necessary permit from the Ministry of High Art and must therefore compose in secret. In his spare time, he attends New Democratic Concerts in which popular classics by the likes of Tchaikovsky are performed alongside the required quota of music by British State-sponsored composers who produce popular items with such names as 'East Purley Serenade' and 'Tone Poem in Praise of the BBC'. Eventually he is undone by one of his co-workers Paul Snigweed who, in turn, he murders before being condemned for the crime of executivicide.

Later Desmond described the novel as a 'prophetic satire on future bureaucracy, too much of which has come true' and while it was quite positively received, *Angels Weep* did not do as well as its more entertaining precursors. Regrettably nor did his fourth work of fiction, *Hold Back the Night*. Once again this shared few characteristics with Desmond's other novels, although its outlook was every bit as bleak as *Angels Weep*. Published in 1956, *Hold Back the Night* is set in a grim, impoverished post-war London where Vernon Field, a young man who wants to become an architect is waiting, rather like John Brown in *Angels Weep*, to receive approval before he can return to university and complete his studies. Vernon has had a nervous breakdown and flashback sections of the novel explain how he has always been in the thrall of his domineering mother. Attempting to escape her control, he once took up with a woman perceived to be 'unsuitable' but was unable to resist parental pressure, leading to an emotional collapse and incarceration in an asylum. Now he has met someone equally inappropriate – not least because she is married – and while on a trip to the country in a car he has stolen, Vernon murders her. He must then dispose of the body, cover his tracks and come up with an alibi. Given his already fragile mental condition, this pressure proves too great for him and the book closes with Vernon rushing into a railway tunnel and towards an oncoming train, imagining he is being reunited with his mother. *Hold Back the Night*'s strengths lie in its depiction of a Britain drained by war and still in the throes of rebuilding herself, of opportunists who exploit any hint of weakness and of encroaching despair. Desmond called it a 'dark horror story which bubbled up from the subconscious … Quite useful to get out of one's system.'

Which leaves the reader speculating about the nature of his own feelings towards Marjorie Leslie, the mother who had so opposed Desmond's marriage to Agnes. None of Desmond's letters to her in adulthood have survived and there is no testimony about how he felt when Marjorie died in February 1951. For many years she had not enjoyed good health, spending periods of time in a nursing home in St Stephen's Green, Dublin. Catching an infection in her kidneys, her condition deteriorated so rapidly that Desmond, along with his brother Jack and father Shane, were all still en route to Ireland from London when she died. 'Her death has occasioned sorrow in many parts of the universe, but particularly at her Glaslough home, where she was loved by all people,' commented a local newspaper. The first Roman Catholic Leslie to be buried on the estate, Marjorie's funeral was attended by a large crowd including the president of Ireland, Seán T. O'Kelly. Seven years later, Shane Leslie would marry again; his second wife was Iris Frazer, herself a widow.

Marjorie's death left Desmond and Agnes slightly wealthier – the latter wrote that they could now afford a nanny for their son Sean – but they were still frequently short of funds. According to Agnes this was why, in 1953, 'Desmond suddenly decided to write a "potboiler". He got interested in various esoteric movements and philosophies and finally developed a passion for the recent phenomenon of flying saucers,' which he thought would make a good subject for a bestseller although Agnes had her doubts. On this occasion she was wrong; as noted in the autobiography of astronomer Patrick Moore – later a good friend of Desmond – in the 1950s 'flying saucers were all the rage'. Reports of sightings around the world became commonplace, leading to a widely held assumption that the Earth was under scrutiny, and very possibly under threat of invasion, from another planet. Desmond had always been fascinated by the idea of alien visitors; as he recalled, one night while at prep school his dormitory had been 'suddenly lit by a brilliant green glare. With yells of delight we rushed to the windows in time to see an immense green fireball move slowly across the sky and disappear behind Sussex Downs. It was so bright that all of the school grounds were lit up in this unearthly green glow.'

Now he started to collect press cuttings from newspapers as diverse as the *Natal Mercury* in South Africa (which suggested that the flying saucers spotted at night were, in fact, a newly developed Russian secret weapon) to the *Japan News* in Tokyo, where there was much speculation on which day the creatures from outer space would choose to land. His interest led him to undertake research into the concept of travellers from outer space and he compiled historical data on the subject, including what he called 'The Flying Saucer Museum', which recorded all visits to Earth made by Venusians, the first being in 18,617,841 BC. The precision of this date was, according to Desmond, 'calculated from ancient Brahmin tables'. Brahmins, he explained, were 'exceedingly accurate people'. He also drew on Celtic mythology, Indian and Sanskrit legend and the Ancient Greek tale of the lost city of Atlantis. Gradually he accumulated a great deal of material which, he believed, all indicated that flying saucers were not a figment of the modern imagination but really existed and had been repeatedly observed by men and women over the previous millennia.

More than a decade afterwards, Desmond wrote of how 'the Venusian aspect was very strong from 1950 onwards. About 1951 I became pottily obsessed with Atlantis, then Egypt, then flying saucers until 1953 when I met Adamski and we looked twice at every visitor in case he was "one of them".'

Desmond with George Adamski, 1954.

A former ice-cream salesman turned mystic, the Polish-born George Adamski had settled in California where he claimed to have seen alien space vessels on a number of occasions. The most notorious of these occurred in November 1952 when, according to Adamski, a large submarine-shaped object hovered over the Colorado Desert after which a smaller scout ship landed and its pilot, a Venusian called Orthon, disembarked to communicate with Adamski via telepathy and hand signals, warning him of the threat of nuclear war. On a later visit, Adamski took a photograph of Orthon's vessel with his telescopic camera although the Venusian declined to be photographed in person. (Adamski did, however, manage to make a plaster cast from Orthon's footprint left in the desert sand. This remains in Castle Leslie.) The image of the Venusian vessel was subsequently dismissed in some quarters as being an altered picture of either a lampshade or a child's spinning top but it was disseminated across the world. Though there had been frequent reported sightings of flying saucers since 1947 none of them was as thrilling or as specific as this and it was suggested to Desmond in England that he might join forces with George Adamski in the United States to co-author a book on the subject.

The two were soon in correspondence and in agreement that, as Adamski wrote to Desmond in early March 1953 on the subject of dealings between humans and Venusians, 'Many contacts preceded mine, but I happened to be the first one "to stick my neck out" by revealing it to the public through newspaper publications. And since then, others have gained the courage to tell me, and others, of contacts made previously to mine.' A month later, Adamski had sent Desmond a manuscript describing his experiences and granted him authorization to act on behalf of them both to see if a book could be published. They agreed that the content should be as follows: the first half would contain Desmond's investigation into the history of flying saucers in global culture while the second offered Adamski's

'Orthon's vessel', taken by George Adamski.

personal account of his experiences including sworn affidavits from a number of his friends as to the veracity of the story. In early May Adamski wrote of his belief that the book would

> do much to clarify the confusion existing in the world today. It is even possible that (it) may be the forerunner of the total truth to come out. For right now it looks as though a great amount of saucer activity will begin either the latter part of this month or in June. So you can picture the effects our book would have in clarifying the minds of the masses if it were to come out somewhere near that time.

In fact the book, *Flying Saucers Have Landed*, did not come out until October 1953 and far from clarifying the minds of the masses it resulted in a great deal of sensationalist and muddled press coverage.

While the fifty-page Adamski account of his personal encounters with the Venusian Orthon was obviously of more immediate popular appeal, Desmond's thorough research into the history of flying saucers – which took up the previous 180 pages – provided a necessary balance and suggested this was a work of serious scholarship. At the same time, he leavened the text with humour. Why don't the aliens land? he rhetorically enquired early in the book before commenting, 'We can only conclude that our planet has a bad name in the stellar year books and travel brochures: like those signs on the roads running through jungles, which caution tourists not to tarry nor leave the safety of their cars. "Warning – Do Not Land on Earth. The Natives Are Dangerous".'

Flying Saucers Have Landed, said *The Observer* in a long feature on the book, 'offers both the enthusiasts and the sceptics plenty of material for controversy'. During the period before and after publication Desmond was extensively interviewed and given an opportunity to present his case. 'You would never guess from looking at him that he is in the forefront of a furore,' began one interview with *Two Worlds* magazine.

> Tall, with the build of an athlete, dark, wavy hair and strikingly good-looking, he is calm, slow of speech and gentle in manner. Yet within the last six months he has startled the public in Britain and America, put half the world's Press agog, confounded scientists, embarrassed governments, bemused at least two air forces and caused more arguments than Senator McCarthy.

Thanks to the popularity of the subject and Desmond's intense publicity campaign, *Flying Saucers Have Landed* proved far more popular than was expected prior to publication, some 250,000 copies being sold within the first year after which it was translated into more than thirty languages and distributed around the world; eventual global sales were around one million. Naturally the book was widely denounced – science fiction author Arthur C. Clarke called the book a 'farrago of nonsense'; Bernard Lovell, Professor of Radio Astronomy at Manchester University, suggested it be 'dumped overboard in space' and *The New Statesman*'s reviewer proposed the only suitable place for *Flying Saucers Have Landed* was 'in the frozen darkness of interplanetary space'. Naturally this criticism only encouraged further public interest. Agnes remembered that as a result of the publicity, 'Desmond now became a household name with the lunatic fringe, and we received letters and phone calls from the strangest of people, including ladies who wanted Desmond to father their children, to create the perfect man. Mediums with messages from Mars were not uncommon.'

It helped that Desmond was prepared to travel and lecture on the subject, giving talks across Britain and Ireland before eager audiences, like the one in Norfolk where he declared that Venusians had been 'very amused' by his book's publication. In Bristol he was welcomed by the British Flying Saucer Bureau but in Dublin, according to *The Irish Press*, he had to engage in debate on Radio Éireann with James Bayley Butler, Professor of Zoology at University College, Dublin and Mr Joe Dillon, who worked in the public relations department of the national airline Aer Lingus. None of this seemed to trouble him. In fact, he relished the attention and was happy to produce still further arguments in favour of the existence of alien visitors. When sceptics mocked that the Venusians had been strangely shy about making their presence known to more than a handful of individuals, Desmond responded, 'Why should they risk a public landing? Their ship would be impounded for evasion of custom duties. Their clothes would be torn off and sold as souvenirs.'

But, he argued, the relevant government authorities were fully aware of alien visitors. In October 1953 he insisted Britain's Air Ministry had been taking the matter 'much more seriously than is known. They have a special department dealing with flying saucer reports, although they would not admit it.' As if to confirm this, a few months later the press reported that another former RAF Spitfire pilot, Colin Hodgkinson, had called a public meeting in London to demand an end to official secrecy on visitors from outer space. 'I have received report after report from the most responsible men in flying that they have seen flying saucers,' he told an interviewer. 'It is ridiculous that RAF red tape should ban serving pilots from making their views on the matter public.' Soon there were widespread sightings, such as that in Norfolk, which took place even before Desmond's visit to the city: two weeks earlier *The Eastern Evening News* announced on its front page that a Mr F.W. Potter of 25 South Park Avenue had observed through the telescope in his garden a flying saucer moving rapidly through the sky.

Excitement over the possibility of alien visitors was equally great in the United States, as was the critical disdain that greeted the publication of *Flying Saucers Have Landed*. 'The book (pardon me while I put on a false beard and phone the police for protection) is one of those outrageous attempts to hype old superstitions with the vital fluid of new scientific discovery,' sniffed the *Chicago Tribune*, which continued, 'It is disheartening that publishers lend their imprint to such junk.' But sales were sufficiently strong to justify Desmond crossing the Atlantic in the summer of 1954 to lecture in a number of cities, including his old wartime haunt Miami, as well as Chicago and Detroit. He also travelled to California to meet George Adamski; hitherto the pair had only communicated by letter. From Adamski's home at Escondido, he sent a telegram to Agnes – at the time appearing in the title role of Oscar Wilde's *Salomé* in St Martin's Theatre, London – informing her: 'Ten Minutes Ago Saw First Flying Saucer So Everyone Happy.' Later that week he wrote more fully from San Diego that he had witnessed 'a beautiful golden ship in the sunset, but brighter than the sunset … It slowly faded out, the way they do.' This was, Desmond would say, the only occasion on which he personally saw an alien craft in the sky. Happy to encourage further book sales, Agnes told the *Daily Mail* that, ' "If all goes well there will be flying saucer landings in England next year …" Those are the words of my husband, Desmond Leslie, written from the Californian desert, where he and an American investigator, George Adamski, are watching the sky in search of flying saucers.'

Back in England after the conclusion of his American tour, Desmond helped to establish a magazine called the *Flying Saucer Review* which half a century later continues to be published. One of his co-founders and fellow contributors was another Anglo-Irishman, the Hon. Brinsley Le Poer Trench, later 8th Earl of Clancarty. The Hon. Brinsley liked to claim he could trace his descent to 63,000 BC when aliens from another planet had landed on Earth. After succeeding to the earldom in 1975 he founded a UFO study group at the House of Lords where his maiden speech was on the subject of flying saucers.

Desmond's fame as a result of *Flying Saucers Have Landed* meant that for several years after its publication he was frequently contacted by journalists looking for good copy. In December 1956, for example, he received an invitation to participate in a live debate on BBC television on the topic of 'Flying Saucers: Do They Exist?' As usual, Desmond made sure the event received plenty of publicity in advance. Two days beforehand, the *People* newspaper reported that at a recent afternoon party in the Leslies' St John's Wood home, Desmond sensed the presence of an alien being who made sure there was sufficient tea and cake for the twenty-eight guests present: 'We all had a cup of tea yet nobody filled the pot and it was still full afterwards!' Assisting Desmond's case on the night of the debate were members of the Royal Astronomical Society and, most impressively, Air Chief Marshal Lord Dowding, the man who had been responsible for the preparation and conduct of the Battle of Britain. What most of the television audience would not have known was that 'Stuffy' Dowding was also a passionate believer in spiritualism and reincarnation, once telling the press baron Lord Beaverbrook that he had been the leader of a Mongol tribe in a previous life. He also claimed to have met dead RAF pilots in his sleep – spirits who flew fighter planes from mountain-top runways made of light. As one of his former staff was to comment afterwards, 'at that stage we thought Stuffy had gone a bit gaga'.

But during the BBC television debate he appeared quite plausible and helped Desmond to win widespread praise for the presentation of his argument that flying saucers regularly travelled to Earth. The case against was argued by young astronomer Patrick Moore who, the *Manchester Guardian* afterwards commented, 'had devilish eyebrows and the fanatical utterance of the born demolishing debater … Desmond Leslie, on the other hand, who is the saucers' leading apologist, was all quiet reasonableness and marshalled his facts and his forces.' Though most press response to the programme was reasonable and tried to see the merits of both sides, the *Daily Mail's* reviewer was irredeemably hostile, observing that 'the presence of Spike Milligan and Peter Sellers would have rounded off the BBC's inquiry into flying saucers, but even without them the programme supplied a fair amount of amateur goonery'. This could have been a reference to the programme's producer who on the night in question arranged to have a camera placed on the roof of the BBC's Lime Grove Studios and pointed skyward, just in case any alien cared to drop by and participate in the discussion.

Desmond remained in touch with George Adamski until the latter's death in 1965. In April 1959, when Adamski was on his way to the Netherlands for a meeting with Queen Juliana (afterwards Dutch Aeronautical Association president Cornelis Kolff declared, 'The Queen showed an extraordinary interest in the whole subject'), he stopped off in London to see Desmond and Agnes who introduced him to their circle of friends. But Adamski's reputation, such as it was, began to decline rapidly later that year when he insisted photographs taken of the far side of the moon by the Soviet lunar probe Luna 3 were fake; instead, he argued, that aspect of the moon contained cities, trees and mountains. In 1962 he announced he would be going to a conference on the planet Saturn and a year later claimed that at the request of extraterrestrials he had held a secret meeting with Pope John XXIII. Nevertheless he and Desmond kept in touch; a letter written by Adamski just two months before he died of a heart attack informed Desmond that since the previous December 'Flying Saucers have been seen daily over Washington DC … it looks from here that this might crack or even tear away the door of silence and let the Dove of Truth free, that all people will know about it.'

Did Desmond himself believe in flying saucers or was it merely, as Agnes proposed, that he had set out to write a money-making pot-boiler? At this distance it's hard to tell which was the case but certainly in public he never apostatized the convictions first publicly stated in 1953. Four years later in an interview with *The Times* he argued that 'reports of flying saucers are absolutely genuine – apart from the crooks and fakes'. This acknowledgement of fraud helped to make Desmond's own certainty appear even more sincere. 'Of course there are plenty of lunatic-fringe reports,' he told another journalist around the same time, 'but even if you dismiss 90 out of every hundred sightings as hallucinations, the remaining 10 are too reliable to be ignored.' In February 1959, various publications reported that Desmond had incorrectly been quoted as saying he thought flying saucers were a hoax. 'I don't know where that story started,' he riposted. 'I've heard it once before but it is completely untrue. My opinions remain quite unchanged.' And in a feature in *Queen* magazine in November 1962 he insisted that

> the inhabitants of other systems have been visiting us for thou-
> sands of years. Elijah was taken up in a flying saucer; the Irish
> hero-god Cúchulain was probably from another world; and the

Angels who came to Abraham at Sodom were physical beings whose description tallies exactly with those we have of Venusians … On Venus there is a human culture roughly 6000 years in advance of our own. They must find current developments here extremely interesting.

Some years after settling back at Castle Leslie, Desmond himself wrote a long feature for a short-lived Irish current affairs magazine called *Scene* in which he once more set out his belief in flying saucers and even argued that they had been sighted in County Monaghan: 'On February 19, 1967 Colm Landers, fifteen-year-old son of Mr and Mrs Brendan Landers and an apprentice joiner at the factory of Monaghan Joinery Ltd, heard a noise which he first thought was a car; but suddenly an object appeared overhead. It seemed about as large as a two-storey house and went over a hill towards the Border.' The possibility that this was an early incursion by a British army helicopter does not seem to have occurred to young Colm Landers, or indeed to Desmond. Interviewed for the same issue of *Scene*, astronomer Patrick Moore – then living in Armagh where he was the first director of that city's Planetarium – said he had known Desmond for a long time 'and I have not the slightest doubt that he is absolutely sincere in what he believes'.

On the other hand, towards the end of his life, Desmond received a letter from Stephen Darbishire, who as a teenager in February 1954 had taken two photographs of what he claimed to be a flying saucer. 'Dear Stephen,' Desmond replied, 'how lovely to hear from you again; you know it's extraordinary that there are still people taking pictures of the old flying saucers … where can they find those 1930s lampshades from, I thought they had all gone out of production.' Was this a tease, or was he finally admitting that his espousal of alien sightings was just a joke? As Stephen Darbishire afterwards said of him: 'You never knew with Desmond. He appeared to believe completely, but he also had a great sense of humour.'

THOUGH HE NEVER wrote another book on the subject, Desmond's interest in the idea of visitors from outer space continued to find expression in several film scripts and synopses he wrote during this period. Twenty-two pages survive of a script called *The Titans*, about John Sturgess, a young prep school teacher who accidentally witnesses a space machine landing in the west of England and takes this information to London and MI5. There he discovers the relevant government authorities have also seen the craft – 'It came from the East and we tracked it crossing our coast at a cool 8,000 miles per hour,' says the Air Minister to whom John gains access with startling ease – but the text ends before the plot advances much further than the hero being reunited with his fiancée. Also extant among Desmond's papers is the synopsis of a television series, *The Venusian*, that he jointly drafted with Agnes and 'Michael Juste'.

The last of these, an Eastern European refugee whose real name was Michael Houghton, had established the occultist Atlantis Bookshop on London's Museum Street in 1922. He also ran an occult lodge, The Order of the Hidden Masters, and was an associate of Aleister Crowley, who had performed black magic rites with Desmond's godfather Evan Morgan at the latter's Welsh home, Tredegar House. Spread over six episodes, *The Venusian* once more involves the arrival in England of a visitor from outer space and the effect this has on everyone he meets, in particular the hostility he encounters from officialdom. It ends with the Venusian dying, 'poisoned by our Earth's atmosphere', after warning the few humans who befriend him that his fellow Venusians 'do not trust you now'.

The Venusian never progressed further than synopsis, but a similar storyline was developed into a script by Desmond and filmed in 1954 as *Stranger from Venus*. This bears more than a passing resemblance to a highly successful film made in the United States three years before, *The Day The Earth Stood Still*, which likewise tells of a visit to Earth

Desmond, 1954.

by an alien who warns mankind of the perils of warfare. As if to point up the parallels, both *Stranger from Venus* and *The Day The Earth Stood Still* shared the same lead actress: Patricia Neal. In the later film she plays an American woman who crashes her car in the English countryside and is resuscitated by an elegant Venusian, the actor Helmut Dantine, whose craft has conveniently landed nearby. The two go to a local inn where the alien reveals his nature and purpose but soon encounters resistance from the humans he meets, other than Patricia Neal who falls in love with him. Desmond's belief that Venusians possessed a more sophisticated and culturally advanced civilization than our own meant the film's conclusion required Helmut Dantine to vaporize after he has been killed. 'By this time, however,' writes one recent admirer of the film, 'the requisite wisdom has been expressed, human foolishness has been exposed and humbled by alien superpowers, and *Stranger from Venus* ends on a quiet note of melancholy optimism.' But it could never hope to compete with the success of *The Day The Earth Stood Still*, made on a much larger budget and liable to attract greater audiences by being set in Washington DC rather than the English countryside. *Stranger from Venus* is today largely forgotten other than by fans of the genre.

So too is Desmond's fifth novel, *The Amazing Mr Lutterworth*, which came out in 1958. As the book opens, the eponymous Mr Lutterworth wakes up on a transatlantic liner on his way to the United States, initially with no idea of who he is or what he is supposed to be doing. Gradually while criss-crossing the continent he comes to understand that he is a visitor to Earth from another planet, temporarily given human form and charged with helping humanity find redemption from strife. The book ends with Lutterworth addressing the United Nations Assembly and sharing out crystals that will bring prosperity and peace to a hitherto disunited world. *The Amazing Mr Lutterworth* received a mixed critical response. *The Observer* summarized it as having 'a very nice beginning, a promising build-up, and a mystical miasma of global salvation at the end', while *The Irish Times* called the novel 'a most unusual and readable piece of fantasy'. On the other hand, in the *Oxford Mail* Brian Aldiss wrote that *The Amazing Mr Lutterworth* 'deals with telepathy in a peculiarly pretentious way … I should have found it unreadable had I not been carried from page to page on a stream of multiple dots, like someone who has stepped on a child's marbles.' It cannot be denied that many of the book's premises are rather far-fetched, not least the notion that a high-flying businessman – in this case called Hasley B. Widlow, vice-president of Global Oil Corporation – would volunteer to a stranger his personal belief in what he calls 'the Great Beyond'. 'I doubt there's a man in my position today,' he elaborates to Lutterworth soon after they have met, 'who's a materialist. No sir, materialism and atheism's a fool's game. Why, even those crooks in the Kremlin have their tame mediums and astrologers … All my friends in big positions know the value of advice from another planet.'

Whatever about Hasley B. Widlow, all his life Desmond was highly susceptible to the concept that there were forms of life other than those apparent on Earth, and to the notion of supernatural spirits. Writing on the subject, he insisted his initial response to séances had been scepticism and remembered that once, when conducting 'a singularly uninspiring question and answer routine with a character who claimed to have lived in Tibet for at least half a million years before his promotion to higher planets, it occurred to me to ask a simple astronomical question: "How many planets are there in our solar system?" "That is a secret," came the reply.' When Desmond then pointed out there were nine known major planets and perhaps three similar yet to be discovered, along with some 5000 minor planets, and that this information was available in any relevant reference book, the spirit 'became rather uncommunicative'.

On another occasion, a spirit, who had seemingly been promoted from Planet Master to Galaxy Master, on being asked how he came to speak such good English, replied, 'My son, we understand *all* your languages.' Unfortunately, someone else at the same séance then posed a question in German 'and there was a dreadful silence'. In other words, Desmond did not perceive himself as naturally gullible or easily fooled.

Nevertheless, he did believe that communication was possible between the living and the dead. In her memoir Agnes recalls an occasion early in their relationship when Desmond dreamt that a Polish pilot who had recently committed suicide appeared before him and wanted to write a message to the world on his arm with a flaming pencil. The following morning, one of Desmond's own arms was a mess of pus and blood spelling out in capitals the word MERDE 'as if they had been carved into his flesh with a knife'. He had an abiding interest in theosophy, the ersatz religious philosophy devised by Madame Blavatsky in the nineteenth century that included among its tenets the notion of universal reincarnation and 'provisional' immortality. In 1957, for example, he described himself as 'a Roman Catholic with theosophical tendencies' and some fifteen years later he told his son Mark that 'I have traced back at least 5 lives which I'm reliving at the moment.'

Desmond was especially impressed by two séances he attended in 1954 in Cardiff. These were presided over by Alec Harris, perhaps the most famous medium of the period. Harris's gatherings were particularly noted for their physical manifestations, with the summoned spirits giving every impression of being present in the room. 'The materialised beings,' wrote Desmond thirty years afterwards, 'could talk, sing and answer questions. They might for all the world have been a group of actors draped in cheesecloth except that (when we were allowed to touch them) their flesh was cold and like the furniture in the room, and one of them dematerialised before our eyes.' On another occasion, Desmond recalled how, at a Harris séance, 'a wonderful Egyptian materialised, took my hands, made me feel his garments, his face and his teeth, and even gave me his name. He was very tall, possibly taller than myself. The other sitters felt sure he was my guide, but I was too awed to ask at the time.' At one of the first séances he ever attended, Desmond had encountered another ancient Egyptian who announced he had been an astrologer during that particular lifetime but reincarnated many times since. When asked to explain why he still appeared as an Egyptian, he laughed and said to Desmond,

> Don't you understand – each life, each incarnation is some-
> thing you create and something that is always your property,
> like a suit of clothes … I happen to find my Egyptian aspect the
> one best-suited to my present work as a spirit guide, so it's the
> one I wear when I come here. In spirit you can pick up and put
> off earlier aspects of yourself as the need arises.

That first trip to Alec Harris in Cardiff had been arranged by a retired British customs officer, Ben Herrington, who at the time was looking after Desmond's flying saucer lecture engagements. The two men travelled to Wales with a Rumanian diplomat, Baron Victor Styrcea, this eclectic little band being typical of Desmond's social circle. Alec Harris and his wife were, it seems, a 'warm and cosy little couple' living in a suburban council house. Here, after some tea and general chat, the séances were held in an upper room where a series of spirits physically manifested themselves, not just the tall Egyptian but also someone who said he had been a scientist in the nineteenth century, described by Desmond as 'intelligent, enthusiastic, with a nice sense of humour, occasionally making a joke'. The scientist invited Desmond to take his hand, which was 'normal in every respect except one. Something was different, some-thing was wrong. *It was the wrong temperature.* Instead of being of normal body heat, it was at room temperature and felt rather like a piece of furniture. That was the difference; every time we handled these entities, I noticed the same difference in temperature …'

On returning to London, Desmond described his experience to Agnes, who immediately asked to be taken to Cardiff. So a second trip was arranged, other members of the party this time again including Victor Styrcea and his wife, as well as two publishers who were interested in the possibility of a book about Alec Harris. The group once more assembled in the small suburban house and were again visited by the nineteenth-century scientist who draped Agnes in ectoplasm that looked and felt like a 'soft, glowing material'. An Egyptian also appeared, as did a Native American, almost seven feet tall and naked other than a small white loincloth, who asked Desmond to pull the glossy black pigtail hanging down his back: 'He seemed to want me to make sure it was no wig, so I gave an enormous wrench which would have hurt any normal person. But the scalp held, and the hair held; nothing came away in my hands.'

Alec Harris claimed to be able to 'dematerialize' himself – to dissolve his physical being in one place and reassemble it in another. Desmond used this idea as material for another unrealized film script, *The Magi*, in which the hero – simply named John – begins as a postulant seeking admission to the White Brotherhood and must undergo various trials and adventures before he is allowed to be initiated into the organization's Inner Mysteries. In one scene, he is confronted with the possibility of dematerialization as his spiritual guide tells him: 'The only thing that prevents you walking through a wall is your physical body ... So we have invented the door [opens it], a bit of wall that disappears and lets us through.' 'But how else could you get through?' asks John, to which his guide responds, 'Like this,' and then walks into the wall, vanishes, is heard in the next room and comes back through the door. Desmond and Agnes's daughter Antonia remembers the couple also attended sessions with Leslie Flint who claimed to possess the rare distinction of being a direct voice medium. This meant that a spirit was able 'to build an ectoplasmic voice box in mid-air rather than speaking through Flint who said he was aware of a presence "a little above my head and to one side of me".'

Desmond later wrote that on one of his visits to Flint, his dead mother was among the entities manifesting themselves to him. Marjorie spoke, 'in a faint voice, saying how hard it was to communicate like this unless you were a spirit guide', but still managed to warn her son 'of a number of events and personalities I was shortly to encounter – everything she said turned out correctly with one exception; this I believe would have happened and was intended to happen, but was frustrated by a last-minute clash of personalities and egos'. Given a recording of another Flint séance in which an entity spoke, claiming to be Edith Cavell, the British nurse shot by the German military during the First World War, Desmond played the tape to his uncle Seymour who told him 'that the voice, intonation and phrasing was absolutely correct for a well-bred woman of that period. Her valedictory sentence was the height of good manners: "I won't be wasting any more of your time, for I'm sure there are far more interesting people waiting to talk to you."'

Many years later, writing about Christ's resurrection in an unpublished work called *What a Way to Run a Universe*, Desmond claimed to have witnessed at least forty complete materializations; 'to have touched, handled and squeezed them, to have conversed with these beings in the presence of many witnesses, all of whom later confirmed identical observations to the exclusion of fraud and hypnotic trickery'.

Desmond's preoccupation with making contact with other worlds – he regularly attended séances conducted by the likes of Bess Hewitson in South Kensington and May Rogers of Nettlefold Green, Sussex – must have served as some kind of escape from his own singularly hectic personal life during these years. Handsome and personable, he found it easy to attract the attention of women and sought every opportunity to do so. It did not take Agnes long to realize that her husband – like his father and grandfather before him – was unfamiliar with the concept of marital fidelity. Her memoir chronicles Desmond's many affairs, which were clearly painful for her to witness since he usually made little attempt to hide them. On one occasion she overheard him arranging a lunch assignation with his current mistress; when the day in question arrived, Agnes rang the restaurant and told the waiter that Mrs Leslie wished to speak to Mr Leslie. There was a pause before the waiter returned to announce, 'Your son says he will call you later, madam.' Amusing as this episode now appears, it must have been intensely unpleasant at the time. Soon the couple were living in an open marriage, with Desmond more inclined to take advantage of this arrangement than Agnes.

'All my married life I was unfaithful,' Desmond once wrote to his sister Anita, explaining that his infidelity was due to a lack of any emotional understanding between himself and Agnes. If this were really the case, then throughout the 1950s he engaged in a great deal of searching to find that elusive emotional bond with another woman. In 1952 he admitted, 'My spirit and my flesh war constantly and are hopelessly intermingled and intermuddled. One day perhaps they'll be straightened out but it's a long, long process.' Desmond's flesh invariably triumphed over his spirit and given the number of affairs he managed to conduct during his twenties and thirties, it comes as a surprise to find him much later insisting that as a young man he had actually been frightened of the opposite sex. This, he said, was because of the religious instruction he had received at Ampleforth where 'I learnt to my dismay that the joyous sap rising in my veins had placed me in appalling danger.' In the June 1968 edition of *Scene* magazine, he wrote how

> when over twenty-one and deeply in love, I succumbed to the horizontal. Now I promise I am not making this up, but the darkness filled with scowling, life-sized crucifixes and glaring patriarchs. I could see them – almost reach out and touch them. Result: all systems at 'No Go'. This kind of guilt-materialisation persisted long enough to make me conclude that I was obviously impotent and that in my retirement to a monastery lay the best solution.

Desmond did not become a monk and he rapidly overcame his fear of women. Quite the contrary, he began to derive immense pleasure from their company – and they from his. According to his daughter Antonia, for most of his adult life Desmond 'didn't want to have any control over himself with women'. Agnes kept note of some of the letters sent to her husband by his mistresses. 'Darling,' declared one in November 1956, 'it was such bliss to have you here again, I never thought it would happen … at least I did not kick you out of bed, I behaved very well and now the old missing you is here again.' Another letter opened, 'Darling fairy story teller, as always you are next to me, like second nature. Why is it that distance doesn't seem to make any difference nor time – I am longing to come back to you, and miss you … how I dream of the day when we are together again, that thought alone makes me patient and calm.'

Even after an affair had ended, Desmond usually managed to remain on good terms with the woman in question and as a rule these relationships had few consequences. One of them, however, proved to be a lot more complicated. Actress Jennifer Phipps was nineteen and had just graduated from the Royal Academy of Dramatic Art when she met Desmond at an actors' party in London. Born in 1932, her mother was a well-known actress. So too was her grandmother, Nancy Price, who also for a time managed the Little Theatre in London's West End and would write twenty-four books of fiction, poems, essays and autobiography. Nancy Price was largely responsible for raising Jennifer since her mother, Joan Maude, was not very interested in the child. Despite being eleven years Desmond's junior, she was something of an independent spirit; they also shared a bond in that her great, great-grandmother had been the famous Swedish soprano Jenny Lind with whom it was widely believed Desmond's great-grandfather Leonard Jerome had been in love (and after whom he was said to have named his second daughter, Desmond's great-aunt Jennie, who died on the day of his birth).

Jennifer Phipps, photo taken by Desmond Leslie, 1952.

Decades later, writing to her son Paul, Desmond remembered his first sighting of Jennifer: 'This blonde vision in a torn cotton top, worn skirt, huge blue eyes and figure to make Marilyn Monroe look flat. We each took one look and what followed could only be described as volcanic.' They began an affair. 'He was a good mentor,' Jennifer would recall. 'I've very fond memories of him although he lived in the clouds, in a world of his own.' But in late summer 1952, Desmond was obliged to come down to earth: Jennifer discovered she was pregnant. When she told Desmond the news, he 'was extraordinarily generous; he opened his arms and held me and said, "My poor darling." ' Nevertheless a decision had to be made about what she should do. By this time, she had met Agnes – then coincidentally also pregnant – who very bounteously suggested Jennifer could come to live with herself and Desmond in St John's Wood. This proposal was soon dismissed as was the notion of Jennifer moving into a cottage in the country. 'Then suddenly,' Jennifer later explained, 'Desmond announced, "I'm going to try something," and went to the phone.'

His call was to the United States, where he spoke to Nelson Jay, commanding officer when Desmond was a trainee pilot in Florida in 1940. The son of a financier who worked for J.P. Morgan, Nelson was born in Wisconsin but had grown up in France and England before studying geology at Harvard University. After the war ended, he had settled in Santa Fe, New Mexico, where he worked for Continental Oil as a pilot and researcher and there in 1951 he married for the second time. Although he had four children from the earlier marriage, he wanted more. Unfortunately his new wife – always called N.C. – was unable to conceive and nor could the couple adopt in their own state; during her own first marriage N.C. had adopted a little boy who was killed in a car accident for which she was held culpable. So on their honeymoon she and Nelson came to Dublin, believing they would be allowed to adopt an Irish baby. Passing through the revolving entrance doors of the Shelbourne Hotel, they had met Desmond who was delighted to be reunited with his old American friend. The Jays quickly discovered they would have to be resident in Ireland for some time before becoming eligible as adopters, so when the honeymoon ended they returned to New Mexico without a baby. But they remained in touch with Desmond, who rang them in November 1952 with the news that a young girl he knew was pregnant. Initially he did not give Jennifer's name and only told the Jays the father of her child was 'my oldest and best friend'. His role, he said, was merely to help the girl find a solution to her dilemma and he had remembered how only the year before the couple were anxious to adopt a baby. Might they be interested in the one Jennifer was carrying? Desmond wrote reassuring them,

> One thing I can guarantee – that it will be a grand baby and much better than one picked from an orphanage. If you agree with me, cable me and I'll cable the girl's name and airmail all the details so you can write to her and get her over. I think you'd like her very much – a very gentle, unselfish person whom I know you'd take to … You must never feel that the actual act of reproduction is so important – whether one can have children or not is only incidental. The important thing is to get the right children into the right homes. You couldn't be more right for

this particular child. Giving it a body is only the beginning. Giving it a LIFE is the big thing.

Further discussions took place before Desmond wrote again, this time providing Nelson and N.C. with both Jennifer's name and her address, and advising them:

> You should write to her there and send her the ticket. I will guide her through the intricacies of the consulate. You should write to her also a letter to show the consul. Dear Jennifer – come and spend the winter with us, etc. A six month stay should suffice … I only pray that I have done the right thing and that this linking of threads will make for wonderful happiness for you and the child now and in future worlds.

Six months pregnant and still only aged twenty, Jennifer travelled on her own to Santa Fe where she moved into the Jays' compound. She brought with her a letter from Desmond in which he admitted at last that he was the expected baby's father.

> I haven't told you this before for several reasons. Main one was that the whole idea was bound to be a bit of a shock to you and I did not want to overflood you with fresh ones – or more than could be assimilated at once. Also I was guided to settle the broad issue first and details later. I am writing this and giving it to Jennifer only in case you wish to know from whom the other side of the child originated. I still half feel it would be better for you never to know, so that you may consider the child to be more of your very own and no one else's. If you know the mother it might slightly detract from this, but if you know the father too it might add to it. I don't, I really don't know. So I am writing anyway just in case, and leaving the rest in the hands of God.

Desmond also made it clear to Nelson and N.C. that he relinquished any paternal rights over the future child, assuring the couple

> positively and irrevocably that from the time you take over I renounce any least feeling of possession or any claim to the tiniest proprietary interest. My interest will be great and I shall love to

hear how the child is progressing, but that will be in the nature of a friend – of one who merely made the introduction. It is your child. No one else's. Please have that quite clear … Whoever he or she is, he will always be in my prayers and I shall take interest in his life, just as the way I would take interest in any good friends of mine.

For Jennifer, young, without friends or family around her and far from home, the weeks leading up to the birth were difficult, particularly since N.C. began to have doubts about whether she and Nelson were entitled to keep the baby. Writing to Desmond on this subject, Jennifer noted that his own correspondence with N.C. had helped to dispel the latter's 'growing and brooding gloom that had been rather alone-making for me, as it was one of those glooms unspoken about but horribly there. It appears that you put straight once again the idea she has that she can't separate mother from child in this manner. Twice we ourselves have discussed this problem …'

Jennifer and Desmond's daughter Wendyl was born in April 1953; only four months earlier in London Agnes had given birth to her and Desmond's second son, christened Christopher Mark but always known by his second name. From Santa Fe, Jennifer wrote to Desmond that their own baby was 'quite the most glorious thing on God's earth. All the others look red, but this one is all ready to move onto a Hollywood set and oust Miss Marilyn Monroe.' Jennifer stayed on another six weeks at Santa Fe caring for Wendyl. Months earlier, she and Desmond had agreed their child would be adopted by Nelson and N.C. but he knew that when the time came for separation she could still change her mind. He had written to his friends beforehand that

the longer she retains her present to you the harder will be the parting. It might be wise for N.C. to take it away immediately to some other part of the States and carry on as if she was the one responsible. Or J. could go to stay with relatives of yours. I think it would be hard for her to go on staying in the same home avec petit l'un. An idea might be for one of you to take her on an exciting tour of various interesting places as soon as she gets up and so take her mind off … I leave it to you though to work out the least painful way of making the change. With your kindness and tact I'm sure you will hit on the best solution. You can discuss everything freely with her.

The eventual parting of mother and baby was, naturally enough, not easy for Jennifer. 'The baby is at the Jays' now,' she told Desmond from Santa Fe. 'I wish it had been possible for you and I to have shared her. However, Fate is very interesting and if it meant me to come to America before I die and this is the only way it could manage it, well … so be it.' Half a century later, she admitted, 'I think I only grew up and lost my heart properly when I left Wendyl.' Eventually it became necessary for her to leave, not least because N.C. was growing steadily more uncomfortable with Jennifer's continued presence. As Desmond had earlier proposed, Nelson gave her the 'exciting tour of various interesting places', took her to California, then across the border to Mexico for a week before he flew her to New York. From there Jennifer caught a ship back to England and resumed her acting career.

In 1958 she met and married a Canadian actor, Peter Boretski and subsequently had two children with him, Paul and Dahlia – Desmond would be the latter's godfather. The Boretskis moved to Canada in 1960 and, other than a short and not very happy spell in Hollywood, remained there enjoying successful careers; Peter died in 2001. Both Jennifer and Desmond stayed in touch with Nelson and N.C. Jay, and with their daughter Wendyl. 'I always knew Desmond as my uncle,' she would say, 'and Jennifer as my unofficial godmother.'

In 1962, on their way to Los Angeles, Jennifer and Peter Boretski spent a weekend with the Jays in Santa Fe and she saw Wendyl for the first time since her birth. Some months later Jennifer wrote to Desmond that their daughter, now aged nine, bore almost no resemblance to her natural mother but was 'a little Desmond walking around the New Mexican plains … she is like one of those women in novels who could walk down her ancestors' hall, and then stopping before a faded old painting of her immediate male ancestor would be looking at herself'. This letter again makes plain Jennifer's regret over the decision she had made in 1953 to leave Wendyl with the Jays but she was also wise enough to understand nothing should be done to alter what had happened, and 'I am sensitively going to leave it at that.' She also realized that her daughter, though still young, was 'worldly-wise and senses more than N.C. believes she does'.

Indeed, according to Wendyl, during that 1962 weekend in Santa Fe she intuitively came to understand Jennifer was her mother but 'I didn't think about who was my father for another year. Then I found out about Desmond and got to know a little about his family. Nelson and N.C. went to a lot of trouble to let me know I was wanted and loved, but to have blood relatives was a whole different ballgame.' Although Desmond had seen her when she was very little and he was on his American flying saucer lecture tour, many years would pass before she met any of the other Leslies, the first being Mark, the half-sibling closest to her in age; they were both twenty at the time, he a Cambridge architecture undergraduate travelling across the United States, she newly married and living in New York. Later she would come to know Antonia and then finally Desmond himself.

In 1984 he and his youngest child Camilla came to spend two days with Wendyl in Saratoga Springs where she was living with her first husband Daniel Beauregard and their two sons Aaron and Matthew – Desmond's grandchildren. 'He took the train and arrived with great flair, a cape across his shoulders. He absolutely stopped the entire railway station.' At one point over the weekend Matthew, then aged five, let out a yell and Desmond announced, 'Oh my God, darling, it's the Leslie shriek!' In 1991 Wendyl and the children came to stay at Castle Leslie and there they met Desmond's other two offspring, Sean and Sammy, and so the circle was complete; along with the rest of his family, Wendyl was with Desmond when he died in the South of France in 2001.

S
E
V
E
N

DESPITE THE JOLT that Jennifer Phipps's pregnancy caused to their marriage, Desmond and Agnes remained together and sometimes even worked on the same projects. One of the latter was *The Missing Princess*, released in 1954. Running to just over half an hour, this black-and-white film told the story of a little princess on a visit to London where she befriends a young boy. Agnes played one of the adult characters, while the part of the princess was taken by a girl called Linda Victoria who does not appear to have acted again. Desmond co-directed along with Alastair Scobie, who was responsible for the script, and the producer was Brendan Stafford; the latter had directed *Stranger at My Door* in 1947 but would later become better known as a cinematographer and television lighting director, most notably for the 1960s cult series *The Prisoner*. *The Missing Princess* didn't lead to further work, and it was around this time that

Desmond announced he was giving up the struggle to make feature films because 'there are easier ways of not earning money'.

Instead, he began considering the possibility of television, as is attested by a number of surviving draft scripts such as that for a comedy, *Miss Wascherbocker's Millions*. Very much in the P.G. Wodehouse vein, the story concerns a Wooster-and-Jeeves pair of characters – in this instance named the Hon. Peter Merryweather and Firebrace – who live in Mayfair and are attempting to raise money to pay off the former's debts before he can marry his girlfriend Lola. Their scheme involves tricking a gullible American heiress into buying paintings hastily run up by Firebrace and summarized in Desmond's script as being 'quite appalling – the newspaper-and-bootlace school mixed with the worst of Picasso's imitators'. When threatened with the possibility of having to run a gallery, Lola tartly declares, 'But I don't want to put on thick glasses and a grey angora jersey in one of those ghastly art shops in the Brompton Road. If we must earn our living, let's open a nightclub.' Nothing came of *Miss Wascherbocker's Millions*, and nor was there much success for another scheme in which Desmond hoped to become involved as a producer: a film based on the life of St Patrick. 'Once in a while,' runs his proposal,

> a Motion Picture is born that is so big in concept, so obviously a box-office 'must' that everyone is surprised it has not been thought of before. Such a Motion Picture is *The Shamrock and the Snake* … The cooperation of the scholars of St Patrick's College, Maynooth, the largest Catholic seminary in the world, has been procured. The film has the full support of the Taoiseach (prime minister) Mr Sean Lemass … Not since *The Robe* has there been a subject so surely conceived to stir the emotions and feelings of the world.

Despite a script by Bridget Boland (a screenwriter whose other credits include *Gaslight*, *War and Peace* and *Anne of a Thousand Days*) and arresting principal characters such as Oona, 'who takes

Agnes in the Castle Leslie drawing room for a magazine feature in 1950.

a vow of chastity when her love for Patrick cannot be returned' and her brother Laoghaire of Tara, 'a champion of paganism and sworn enemy of St Patrick and Christianity', *The Shamrock and the Snake* remains unmade to this day.

There was, however, one area of film work in which Desmond now started to enjoy some success: music scores. His career as a composer began inadvertently in 1947 when funding for *Stranger at My Door* ran out before the soundtrack had been composed. According to Agnes, Desmond bought reels of music from various libraries and then edited them together 'by playing some of these tracks backwards or re-recording them on top of one another until he had achieved the desired effect. The music turned out to be almost the best thing in the film.' Desmond had always been a fine pianist, able to sight-read music scores and to improvise on an instrument. And his 1948 novel, *Angels Weep*, is full of descriptions and analyses of music by a wide range of composers. Inevitably, however, when it came to his own work traditional forms of composition did not appeal and he felt the need to adopt an entirely new approach to the process. After *Stranger at My Door* was finished, he continued to experiment with taped reels of music and arranged for Rupert Neve, a sound engineer who would later become Britain's leading designer of recording equipment, to build him a mixing console on which he could more easily compose. The spare room in the St John's Wood flat was turned into a studio containing – in addition to the mixing desk – four tape recorders, two amplifiers, an echo chamber, microphone, piano and an extensive library of tapes. These contained thousands of different sounds: as a report in *The Times* noted in July 1962, they included 'people marching, birds singing, bombs exploding, lathes turning, storms raging, cars starting'. Agnes remembered how he would 'use these sounds as a painter would use the colours on his palette to create sound "pictures" and ended up with whole symphonies'. This was what Desmond called 'musique concrete'.

On the jacket of *Music of the Future*, a long-playing record he released in 1960, Desmond called musique concrete an 'untranslatable term for the arrangement and selection of sound patterns into an intelligent, evocative and potent new musical form'. Or, his seven-year-old son Mark was quoted as saying in an article on Desmond published in August of the same year, 'Daddy records the tide coming in, plays it backwards and says it's the tide going out.' Two years later, Desmond elaborated on the character of musique concrete, explaining that while 'in ordinary music one can and usually does identify the source of each sound', the same was neither possible nor desirable with his compositions.

> One should not be thinking 'This is brass. This is string.' One's whole attention should be on the sound for its own value. One of the advantages of electronic music is that it is pure sound. As it relates to no recognisable source it exists in its own dimension and is capable of exerting fully its conscious and subliminal impact without the usual string of conditional references in the mind of the hearer.

Desmond sold many of the pieces he created through London music publisher Joseph Weinburger as incidental music for films, stage plays, advertisements and television programmes; some of his work was even used in early episodes of the BBC's first *Doctor Who* series. For a while he formed a partnership with the writer and critic Simon Harcourt-Smith, whom Agnes disliked, describing him as 'the sort of flawed character to whom Desmond was always fatally attracted'.

But aside from this relatively brief collaboration, Desmond worked alone. Among the commissions he received was a soundtrack to *The Death of Satan*, a satirical play by Ronald Duncan, remembered as librettist of Benjamin Britten's 1946 opera *The Rape of Lucretia* and scriptwriter for the 1968 film *Girl on a Motorcycle* starring Marianne Faithfull. In his programme note for the piece, Desmond announced that he had 'abandoned satire for

James Stevens, and his mystical poem of the redemption of Satan where the Universe is rolled up and his terrible work is done. Thus the composition consists of Descent-Inferno-Danse-Dantesque-Death of Satan-Bells of Heaven.' In 1959, Desmond composed the score for *The Day The Sky Fell In*, a fifteen-minute film written and directed by Barry Shawzin, which was shown at the following year's Venice Film Festival where it was described as 'the first feature film in miniature' and caused a considerable stir. A parable on the threat posed to the world by the proliferation of nuclear weapons, Desmond considered *The Day The Sky Fell In* to be 'the perfect film on which to graft my sounds'. His enthusiasm for the film could, at least in part, have been because its underlying message reflected his own views. Early in *The Amazing Mr Lutterworth*, while still crossing the Atlantic, the protagonist learns that scientists have invented the atomic bomb and asks:

> But why do that? There is more power in the free air in this room, power that is safe, creative, positive than in all the uranium in the world. It's the wrong approach. It's like burning down your house to boil an egg, like trying to fire this ship across the ocean with a huge gun. It's the wrong application. It's negative. Positive force is creative, silent, safe. Negative force is abrupt, violent, wasteful and destructive. They must be insane!

Both Desmond and Agnes had become involved with the Campaign for Nuclear Disarmament soon after this organization was established in late 1958 and on the roof of their St John's Wood flat they even set up an anti-bomb pirate radio station run by Bertrand Russell and Vanessa Redgrave. They took part in a number of protests and marches including a gathering in Trafalgar Square in September 1961. Organized by the radical wing of CND, the Committee of 100, this had been banned by the government. Nevertheless 15,000 members of the public turned up before the assembly was dispersed by the police and most of the key figures arrested.

Desmond was among the latter, Agnes remembering that it took six members of the police force to drag him into the waiting Black Maria. He spent the night in prison, sharing a cell with Vanessa Redgrave, jazz musician George Melly and playwright Shelagh Delaney. The following morning he returned home where, according to a report in the *Daily Express*, he was greeted by eight-year-old Mark with a sign declaring 'Ban the Bed'.

The following February his name was again in the newspapers after he wrote to both the American and Soviet presidents suggesting they forget their political differences and unite in a joint programme of space research. 'My idea,' he told the *Daily Express* reporter, 'is that when the two countries go ahead with two-man spacecraft, the Russians should carry an American astronaut as a passenger, and vice-versa.' It would be some time before this proposal came to be implemented. Meanwhile in May 1962, after the leader of the Labour Party, Hugh Gaitskell, accused CND of being infiltrated and controlled by communists, Desmond started a letter-writing campaign to the press, insisting that 'CND in fact is infiltrated by Catholics, Protestants, Jews, Marxists, Tories, Socialists, Liberals; in fact by everyone who takes Einstein's warning seriously and who objects to the idea of a third generation being born with two heads, three legs and no mind (and possibly no soul).'

Not that Desmond was averse to stirring up a little disharmony, albeit on a less-than nuclear scale and strictly within musical parameters. Listeners to his *Music of the Future* album were advised, 'Put this record on a good Hi-Fi set. Twiddle the knobs till you find the levels you like. Tell the neighbours to go to hell (they'll probably only think it's the plumbing). Sit back and enjoy yourself. My MUSIQUE CONCRETE is meant to be enjoyed.' Re-released in 2005, the album was described by a critic for *Stylus* magazine as being 'not forbidding or austere but raw and alive, with strong rhythmic motivation', the aspiration expressed that this particular selection of pieces 'will hopefully establish him in the slowly growing pantheon of UK electronic music pioneers'.

It cannot be claimed that, on hearing Desmond's music, everyone has been equally enthusiastic. In May 1958, the *Daily Express*'s William Hickey column reported on a party in the Leslie home where 'Miss Dorothy Meynell, who is Lady-in-Waiting to the Duchess of Gloucester, placed two fingers in her ears and said, "Gosh! I never heard such a din".' Desmond had been playing one of his compositions, derived from the sound of aircraft taking off and landing but so transformed by him that 'The year is 2060; the scene London Airport. A rocket is about to leave for the moon. This is what you will hear.' Almost two years later the Londoner's Diary in the *Evening Standard* noted that Desmond had unintentionally created some more musique concrete and received a summons from the police for his efforts. The fault lay with his car: 'The silencer tends to come off,' Desmond explained. 'It makes a more interesting noise that way.'

Happily not all of his music had quite such an aggressive sound. One of the pieces he wrote during these years was the punningly titled *Concerto in Bee*, featuring the sound not only of a piano but also of bees, flies and other insects. The work had four movements beginning with an allegro called 'The Hot Summer Meadows'. This was followed by a scherzo, 'Argument between Determined Piano and Angry Horse-Flies' and then came an andante, 'The Primeval Forest', before the concerto closed with a finale.

Desmond received his most important commission in the spring of 1962 when His Master's Voice invited him to compose soundtracks for twelve of Shakespeare's plays. These were being recorded at the time with the likes of John Gielgud and Ralph Richardson in *Othello*, Michael Redgrave in *Macbeth* and Vivien Leigh and Peter Finch in *Anthony and Cleopatra*. Before Desmond began work on the project, Rupert Neve designed a new mixing desk for him, named the Electronic Musical Stereo Compositor. He was using the desk when *The Times* visited him in his studio in July 1962, composing music for *The Tempest*, which featured Donald Wolfit as Prospero. 'Listen to this,' Desmond instructed the reporter as he adjusted some dials. 'Isn't that a wonderful sound? Basically it's the noise of a wasp's nest with electronic amplification.' In his sleeve notes for the twelve recordings, Desmond argued that owing to its timelessness, musique concrete was

> an ideal backing for great classical literature which is also time-less. In Shakespeare's day the finest sound that could be pro-duced was the English language itself; it was therefore in words rather than instruments that composers expressed themselves … Shakespeare, I am sure, would have welcomed musique concrete. His very stage directions not only bristle with excel-lent musical and realistic sound: 'Solemn and strange music', 'Flight Alarum', 'Ordnance Off', but show a keen ear for ster-eophony with frequent indications that the sound should come from left or right, near or distant, all of which is now possible with twin channel recording systems.

Since the recordings had no visual accompaniment, Desmond advised,

> I have tried to replace the scenery, the lighting and the staging of the players with sounds intended to evoke huge visual pano-ramas in the mind of the listener. To do this I use both abstract sounds intended to convey a mood, a colour or an emotion and also recognisable sounds such as galloping horses, echoing footsteps, swishing clanging swords and cries of battle. These I mix carefully so as to give a visual and a mood picture.

There is no doubt that the *Living Shakespeare* series was Desmond's most important commission to date and ought to have led to many more. In fact, given his early proficiency in electronic music, he should have enjoyed future success as a film and television composer in the years ahead. But that was not to happen because in 1963, after eighteen years of living in London, Desmond returned to Ireland to assume responsibility for his family estate.

EIGHT

FOUR YEARS HAD PASSED since a tearful separation from his family and Cruiskeen Lawn, his home and domain on the Irish border. He began to think of it now, those groves of huge trees, interwoven with shining lakes, their edges brushed by willows that leaned over in the wind and stirred the green water, and the amber pools where in sunlight the fish lay basking.

In his 1946 novel, *Pardon My Return*, Desmond's description of Rory Headstone's arrival at Cruiskeen Lawn provided the author with an opportunity to express his own feelings for the place that served as a model for the fictional estate: Castle Leslie. Not long after returning home, Rory stands on the terrace,

watching the sunset light up the lake. Pastels swam in infinite subtlety; no vulgar colours when an Irish day meets its end. The lake had become a sheet of mother of pearl, emphasising each delicate shade in every little ripple … The lake had changed again. Only the palest of green remained, varied by a grey that could only be so called for lack of a more suitable adjective. A moment before it had been the last remnants of peach, shortly it would become the most furtive of blues, but now midway between the two, it had to be called grey.

Rory's love for Cruiskeen is so great that it matches, possibly even surpasses, his feelings for Thistle Conlon, the 'unsuitable' girl he wants to marry. 'He knew that he was part of Cruiskeen. The roots were eternal. He dearly loved Thistle, but his love could never be complete until she could share Cruiskeen, his home.' This was how Desmond felt about Castle Leslie. 'To me,' he said in a 1996 television interview, 'this place is a dream – the most beautiful place in Ireland … an absolute paradise.'

'An Irish childhood,' his sister Anita declared in her memoir, 'does something to one's toes, causing invisible roots to grow into the soil.' In 1963 Desmond responded to his Irish roots. As he wrote from Castle Leslie in April 1983 to his older brother Jack,

> 20 years ago I decided I wanted to settle down here at lovely Glaslough and never move again, and by every means in my power try and preserve the best part of it. From that resolve I've never wavered nor had second thoughts … I had to sacrifice my exciting career as an avant garde composer (at which I was earning today's equivalent of £50,000) and forget it all to save this estate. But I would not do any otherwise, had I the choice over again.

Desmond's reasons for coming to live at Castle Leslie were complex and need to be explained. Shane Leslie having renounced his birthright, the estate had been bequeathed by Sir John Leslie to Shane's son Jack, who lived there after being released from a German prison camp in 1945. Jack's inheritance was contained within a legal entity, the Sir John Leslie Estate Company, of which he was the major shareholder. It owned all the land, houses and their contents. But in 1953, two years after his mother's death, Jack in turn relinquished his ownership of Castle Leslie and moved to Rome where he would remain for the next forty years. Shares within the Sir John Leslie Estate Company were now divided between Anita and Desmond, with the former holding a slightly larger quantity. And since Desmond was living and working in London, the actual management of Castle Leslie and its farm fell to Anita and her husband Bill King, and they took to dividing their time between Counties Monaghan and Galway, where they had restored Oranmore Castle. During the summer months Desmond and his family would travel from England to Glaslough and take up residence in the house but they had almost nothing to do with running the place and keeping it on a secure financial footing. This scenario continued for ten years.

However, by 1963 the Kings were justifiably no longer happy with the status quo and informed Desmond a change would be necessary. They were finding it harder and harder to make the estate pay for itself; indeed, Castle Leslie had begun to lose money. A letter written in July 1959 from the estate manager to an English associate of Desmond who had taken interest in the place noted, 'I have not received the Auditor's account and balance sheet yet, but the Accountant informed me that he estimated the loss on the estate this year would be £9000.' Desmond tried to help, but his interventions tended to lead to disaster. In 1956, for example, a large quantity of timber from the estate was sold for the considerable sum of £53,000 and Desmond decided to lend the money raised from this transaction to a Dublin businessman, Gerard Counihan, who offered land in Wicklow as collateral on the loan. Unfortunately, the land turned out to be rented and three years later Counihan was declared bankrupt; meanwhile Bill King had undertaken improvements on the Castle Leslie farm in the expectation that he would eventually be able to pay for them with the money raised in 1956. When this proved not to be the case, some parcels of land and a number of artworks from the house had to be sold to raise the necessary funds. It was a situation destined to be repeated on a number of future occasions because, as Agnes had observed, Desmond had exceedingly poor commercial skills and was forever attracted to flawed characters with whom he became entangled in schemes of questionable merit.

Trying to keep Castle Leslie solvent took up a great deal of the Kings' time and energy and, naturally enough, they found this difficult to accept since they were only co-owners of the property. In 1963 they announced they had had enough and issued an ultimatum: either they would be allowed to take over full responsibility for Castle Leslie or they would hand the place over to Desmond. In April Anita wrote to her brother that she had discussed the matter with Bill King

> and he said he just would not bear to slave all through the year for a place that was not his home and be expected to move out for any part of the summer holidays when he likes to be tranquil and alone with his family … If he has to clear out of the house at all he would rather clear out *completely* & I think it best for us all this should now take place … I really think it might be best this year if I myself roll up the company in July, pay the house expenses during August … and make it all over to you Sept. 1st, Bill relinquishing before then.

The following month she commented that 'For 100 years the main drains have been neglected & the walls allowed to decay. Present situation: Bill has made it clear (a) that he is not willing to continue joint ownership and (b) we are I think in agreement on the roll up of the company which is now solvent.'

What was to happen next? Desmond prevaricated for some months, not least because his own career as a composer had begun to show signs of success. So too had that of Agnes as a performer.

Throughout the 1950s, she appeared in a wide variety of productions – everything from performing as the first non-stationary nude on the English stage (in Oscar Wilde's *Salome*) to playing Scheherazade in a lavish pantomime of *Aladdin* at the London Palladium. But in the spring of 1963, just as Anita and Bill were requesting her husband to make a decision over the future of Castle Leslie, she was given the opportunity to stage a one-woman show in the West End. Based around the songs of Bertolt Brecht and Kurt Weill, *Savagery and Delight* was booked to run for three weeks at the Duchess Theatre. It had a disastrous opening night because Desmond had forgotten to install the speakers intended to project Agnes's voice and she could not, therefore, be heard any further than the first couple of rows in

Agnes nude as Salome, 1956.

the auditorium. The critics took their own delight in being savage, with Bernard Levin writing a particularly ferocious review in the *Daily Mail*.

Perhaps because he was to blame for the microphone mishap and as a balm to his guilty conscience, Desmond took umbrage at Levin's remarks and accordingly, the following Saturday evening while Agnes was on stage at the Duchess Theatre, her husband went to the BBC television studios from where the satirical show *That Was The Week That Was* was being broadcast live. Bernard Levin was among the programme's regular presenters and had barely sat into his place than Desmond stepped out of the audience. 'One minute, Mr Levin,' he said. 'Before you begin, it won't take a minute. Would you stand up a second? Mr Levin, your review of *Savagery and Delight* was not a review; it was a vicious attack.' 'Yes, it may well have been,' responded a clearly bemused Levin who then suggested, 'Would you mind going back?' 'There's just one tiny thing to be done,' said Desmond, before lunging with a punch at the critic in front of an estimated 11 million television viewers. As Levin picked himself off the floor, Desmond was led out of the studio – by a young David Frost – a smirk of delight visible on his face. Watching the episode in retrospect it all seems remarkably civilized with both men smartly dressed in suits and ties and – until Desmond threw his punch – each addressing the other in the era's polite, well-modulated tones.

Subsequently described in *The Times* as 'the most public punch since Sonny Liston took the heavyweight title from Floyd Patterson', Desmond's behaviour caused a sensation and was given first place in a 2001 BBC listing of 'Top-Ten TV Bust-Ups' as well as being recalled in every obituary following Levin's death in August 2004; the scene has since been made available on YouTube. Naturally the incident was picked up by the foreign press, where it was often incorrectly reported as being a crime passionelle. At the time, Irish actor Micheál MacLiammóir – then in London with his new one-man show *I Must Be Talking to My Friends* – wrote, 'Darling Desmond! Never thought of you in the role of a pugilist I must say! You grow in interest every day. It really was splendid of you and Agnes must have felt you were defending her at the risk of your life! What brutes are critics, and now what critics many brutes are ...' Likewise from Oranmore, Anita let Desmond know, 'Galway enchanted with newspaper accounts of your exploit – they've never heard of Brecht or Bernard Levin but feel it such a good thing anyone would punch anyone over his wife's voice!'

Proving the maxim that there's no such thing as bad publicity, Agnes benefited from Desmond's televised display of uxoriousness and once her run at the Duchess Theatre came to an end she found herself being offered further work and even the possibility of an American tour. Under these circumstances, she had no desire to leave London and settle in the Irish countryside. Desmond continued to dither and thereby irritate Anita and Bill King who were pressing for a definite response to their request that either he or they assume total responsibility for Castle Leslie. They offered to buy out his share of the estate for £20,000 and, having rejected this proposal with seeming firmness, he changed his mind. 'Your letter arrived as rather a bombshell to Bill,' Anita told him in mid-May,

> He had certainly understood on your last talk in London that you did not accept his offer of £20,000 and when he came back, said, 'Well, at least it is settled. I have shot my bolt and Des has made his decision clear to me' ... He is really bouleversé by your letter and wants a fortnight to collect his wits and readjust his already readjusted plans.

Desmond then changed his mind again and announced that, regardless of the money being proposed, he could not relinquish all interest in the family home. 'Why do people hang onto their castles and estates against all odds?' he had asked in a feature written for

Picture Post in April 1950 before explaining, 'Because one has grown to love it. That's why. Some things cannot be measured in terms of council statistics and modern finance.' Anita also dearly loved Castle Leslie, but she was more practical-minded than her younger brother and pushed for a conclusion to be reached according to which just one of them would assume entire responsibility for the estate.

Although he had no stake in the matter, their septuagenarian father now also became involved, writing from London to his daughter: 'Desmond cannot make offers by starts and darts. All is very unsatisfactory … It would be wise to accept a good compromise for the sake of the family. You three children were given everything before your time and now you must all make sacrifices so that all four [grandchildren] will have a division of heritage as well as what they can share together.' The following month he told Desmond, 'I have had huge correspondence with Anita and Bill over Glaslough and I sincerely hope you will make a final and friendly agreement for the future this autumn … I have instructed a pauper's funeral for myself – no coffin or expenses, no undertaker – only low Mass. But I leave my four Glaslough pictures to whoever saves the place.'

One of Desmond's suggestions was that he be permitted to retain a section of the house for his own use. Castle Leslie was certainly big enough to allow for this arrangement; Seymour Leslie and his wife Timmie (and later their daughter Jennifer) were already living in one wing. But, he explained to Anita, 'having two sons complicates it. I could not properly sell their birthright without their full consent, so I asked Bill to wait a little while.' The Kings, however, had grown tired of waiting and insisted an irrevocable decision be made. Finally it was agreed that in lieu of their share of the Castle Leslie estate they would keep Drumlargen, a prosperous farm in County Meath that had been bought with capital left by Jack when he moved to Italy ten years before. Desmond would take over full responsibility for the family home, demesne and farm. 'I understand that October 1st 1963 is the transfer date,' wrote Bill King in a memorandum. 'It is hoped that the place will be solvent at that time, all large debts, death duties, mortgage, Agricultural Credit Corp., etc. paid off and the bank balance about level, up or down a little.'

And so, in autumn 1963 the Sir John Leslie Estate Company was wound up and Desmond assumed control of Castle Leslie, his home for the following thirty years. Initially he came to live there without Agnes. She was still very reluctant to leave London and viewed the move to Ireland 'with much anguish and apprehension'. But in any case, for the moment she could not travel: that spring Agnes had discovered she was once again pregnant but there were complications and she was advised to remain in London until after the birth; Antonia Leslie was born in St John's Wood on 1 November 1963.

Desmond and Agnes with Antonia at the latter's christening, 1963.

Afterwards, Agnes stayed for another few months because the lease on the flat had to be given up, its contents packed and sent across to Ireland. Only in late January 1964 did she take a ferry to Belfast before driving to Glaslough with her daughter. 'It was a route I had taken many times before, always in a happy holiday mood,' she wrote in her memoirs. 'This journey was different. While my baby slumbered peacefully, my feelings of doubt and apprehension grew with every mile we put behind us.'

Agnes was right to feel concern for the future. Unlike his brother-in-law Bill King, Desmond was temperamentally unsuited to be a farmer and nor had he the qualities needed to make a good businessman, especially given the very difficult circumstances he would have to face. He had spent the two previous decades in London writing and composing, activities for which he was naturally suited and from which he had derived enormous pleasure and a fair measure of success. Taking over an impoverished Irish estate was never going to be an easy task, no matter how great his love for the place.

Desmond in the mid-1960s.

Owners of such properties could expect no support from the State. As Desmond had remarked when writing in *Picture Post* in 1950, Ireland at the time suffered from 'a hopelessly illogical system of rates. English tax at least taxes earnings. Irish rates tax a piece of land whether it earns or loses, and to many, even small farmers, this means ruin.' Furthermore, the government's Land Commission was forever looking for opportunities to buy out large estates, often on injurious terms for their owners, and to divide the acreage between small farmers. The 1950s and 1960s were difficult times for many Irish estates and very few of those in the vicinity of Castle Leslie would survive.

But Desmond convinced himself that he had a sacred obligation to keep the estate within the family. As he told his son Sean in May 1975, 'I have been solemnly charged to preserve Glaslough and to turn it into a sanctuary for the future … I have been told, "You have planted an acorn which can grow into a mighty oak, and your children and their children may carry on the work".' Eleven years earlier, he – and Agnes – approached the task of ensuring the estate's survival with gusto, flair and imagination. By early 1965 Desmond had come up with three schemes for Castle Leslie, one of which was that a factory be established within what had been the old grain loft and machine workshops of the home farm. In a television programme about Glaslough made a year later, writer and broadcaster Bruce Arnold observed that the area was becoming depopulated through emigration to Britain or the United States: 'Flax has vanished from hillsides and valleys and with it employment for many people,' he remarked. 'Lace-making is gone and there is little employment on any of the estates.'

Desmond proposed setting up an embroidery and hem-stitching factory in the grounds of Castle Leslie, arguing that up to fifty workers could be trained within the first year and a further fifty during the next two. The raw material would be brought to County

Monaghan from Northern Ireland, where there was greater industry but a shortage of competent staff. At the Castle Leslie factory, this material could be processed and finished as handkerchiefs and scarves, and then sent back across the border. 'The proposed operation seems a sensible one,' argued Desmond in a document setting out his proposal. 'The demand exists. County Monaghan has the labour, Glaslough has the right premises.' Sadly, though, no one had the necessary funds and government support was not forthcoming, so the plan came to naught. Meanwhile Desmond had come up with another idea, this one to utilize a large stone building that stood just inside the main gates of the estate. Originally the agent's house, it had briefly served as a residence for Daughters of the Holy Ghost nuns while Jack still lived in Ireland but was now empty.

Desmond thought the property might serve either of two purposes, the first being as a luxury private health centre and spa run by two naturopathic doctors, Chandra Sharma and Leonard Symonds, who had been 'seeking a place of rare natural beauty, absolute peace and quiet, with air completely free of industrial pollution, remote enough to be in "another world" yet not so far as to be inaccessible'. That place was the old agent's house at Castle Leslie, which alternatively could be transformed into 'an ideal home of well-to-do old people under an endowment scheme'. In other words, it would become a smart retirement home. 'I understand a number of such schemes are under way in England and America,' Desmond wrote to one potential financial backer. 'Large country houses with their resident nurse and visiting doctor forming an elegant setting for old people who have been used to a gracious way of life, but who are now alone, or who wish to disencumber their children but who would love to be able to go on living in the old style of space and comfort.'

Many of Desmond's proposals were extremely far-sighted and would later become widespread but at the time none of them advanced very far before reaching the same insurmountable obstacle:

lack of capital. The draft proposal for converting the former agent's house and its outbuildings into a thirty-bed health centre, for example, shows the anticipated cost of this job to have been £21,000. While some government grant aid might have been forthcoming, private investment would have had to provide most of the money. In the insolvent 1960s, that kind of support was just not available. Forty years later, when the country had grown altogether more prosperous, Desmond's daughter Sammy would finally accomplish what he had not.

Disappointed to find his various propositions thwarted, Desmond opted to turn the agent's house – which had hitherto been promoted on the basis of its 'absolute peace and quiet' – into Ireland's first rural nightclub. Annabel's on the Bog opened in 1966, its name taken from Mark Birley's already famous premises in London. On the opening night, an elderly local man approached Desmond and declared, 'Congratulations Mr Leslie. At last you've brought sin to Monaghan.' When Bruce Arnold and his television crew visited Castle Leslie that year, they interviewed Desmond, resplendent in white dinner jacket and bow tie, inside the club where he was filmed playing Cole Porter's 'Night and Day' on an electric organ before the scene switched to show dancers gyrating to the sound of more contemporary rock music. Talking to Arnold, Desmond said he thought the building 'would make the most wonderful country club … the first thing we did, because it was the quickest and easiest and I had all the sound equipment, was to make a discotheque and restaurant'. But, he explained, his plans were by no means finished. Annabel's on the Bog was 'just the beginning, the trailer, so to speak. The 12 rooms here will be refurbished, they'll be properly residential. There'll be a waterski club and sailing club on the lake … and then I want to turn that lovely old stableyard into a holiday lodge.'

Though it attracted considerable publicity, Annabel's on the Bog did not survive a year. Since it was a private club and not subject to the laws governing pubs and hotels, Desmond was not bound by the usual licensing laws. On the other hand, the influential local Catholic clergy were hostile and made their views known; when Bruce Arnold asked one young woman, identified only as Ann, what she thought of the idea of dancing in the club after midnight, she paused and then giggled nervously before responding, 'I think it's a problem.'

Desmond in dinner jacket at his nightclub, Annabel's on the Bog, Ireland's 'first rural nightclub', 1960s.

Post-midnight dancing wasn't Desmond's only problem. As had been the case throughout the years in London, he was living beyond his means but now his outgoings were very much greater. Though the estate was just about solvent, after Anita and Bill King's departure, the loss of the County Meath land meant it had no financial reserves on which to draw should any difficulties arise. Desmond had never been sensible with money and by 1966 he was heavily in debt to a number of lending institutions. As he recalled to Jack fifteen years later, one bank then tried to foreclose on the estate and would have succeeded except that his solicitor 'raised countless, often frivolous, objections, asking for adjournment after adjournment – 38 in all I believe! … This went on for two or three years giving me time in the end to find the money and pay them off.' Admitting that he had not had 'a single leg to stand on', Desmond acknowledged what he had needed was sufficient time and that his solicitor had gained this 'by simple legal filibustering and finagling. And it worked. I STILL HAVE GLASLOUGH.'

He was going to rely on a lot more filibustering and finagling over the next couple of decades. It didn't help that – other than holding on to Castle Leslie – Desmond was never altogether sure what he wanted. In August 1965 Noel Gabriel, an English lawyer who had been advising Desmond on the health clinic scheme, let the Glaslough estate accountant know:

> It has come to my ears that (just as I had suspected) Mr Leslie has been in communication with me on the one hand, but has been simultaneously negotiating with others in an entirely different direction and on an entirely different footing. This does not surprise me in the least as I felt sure that the very obvious confusion in his mind on practically all the occasions when I discussed matters with him must be down to the fact that he was trying to examine more than one possibility at the same time … so far he has seemed to have some difficulty in getting down to earth – and if I may say so not unkindly has been in a

slightly alarming situation in the clouds owing to the fact that he seems to have a foot in each of two clouds simultaneously, if not more!

Desmond's next idea was to develop a hotel inside the Castle Leslie demesne. The main house stands on rising ground above a lake, at one end of which lie the nineteenth-century walled gardens built as a sequence of terraces with the land descending eastwards and terminating not far from the water's edge. By the late 1960s, without staff to maintain them, the gardens had been largely abandoned but now Desmond came up with the concept of a hotel within their walls. It would have the advantage of being inside the estate but not visible from the main house, where he and other members of the family could continue to live.

Not everyone shared his enthusiasm for the project. In September 1968 Anita wrote: 'I *hate* the idea of a hotel in the garden but if this is the only method you can find of raising money I suppose you will have to sell it ... But whatever happens, do not sell land bordering on the lake or give the hotel access to the boat house except under your supervision.' The proposed five-star hotel's design was actually rather ingenious and took full advantage of the site and the prospect it offered. Conceived by a French architect called Florent Margaritis – described in a later prospectus as being 'best known for some of France's more gracious public buildings and a number of beautiful private homes on the Riviera' – the building would have nestled into the garden's existing configuration. As Desmond informed his son Sean in August 1968,

> All you will see from the lake is a series of beautiful landscaped terraces, hung with plants and vines (in the lower part of the garden below the hedge) these are in fact the bedrooms, in three terraces with the roof of each below forming a lawn and patio for the one above. Very subtle. Above the hedge, where the greenhouses stand, there would only be a single, graceful

building, mainly glass, wood and climbing vines, containing the public rooms and looking like a beautiful garden pavilion.

Writing about the project, Margaritis explained it had been the 'unusual silence, the everlasting yet ever-changing spectacle unfolded by nature against a background of Glaslough Lake and the forest on its banks, and also the splendid, inimitable and matchless hedges that Mr Desmond Leslie's grandfather so fortunately planted, which have guided me in choosing the course of action … A tiered hotel "just like a theatre".' Access to the hotel was to be via one of the estate gates within Glaslough village so that guests would arrive at the top of the walled garden and be greeted by the unparalleled prospect of lake and woods spread before them.

Gradually the hotel proposal became more grandiose, with the addition of a private sporting club based around a 350-acre golf course to be designed by Robert Trent Jones, at the time probably the best-known practitioner in this field. By the early 1970s Desmond had produced a lavish brochure offering membership to the club, which included among its founder life members an impressive list of grandees such as the Dukes of Bedford and St Albans, Prince William of Gloucester, and – closer to home – Irish peers like the Earls of Caledon and Mount Charles and the Hon. Desmond Guinness. Writing in the same brochure, Robert Trent Jones declared himself to be 'as enthusiastic about this new golf course as I am about the whole project, for like everything else in this enchanted demesne it has a special quality that convinces me that it will soon become recognised as one of the world's "Greats" '. But the recognition never came about because the project, like so many of both its predecessors and successors, remained unrealized. Work was begun on the course and a site levelled for the clubhouse until the Northern Ireland Troubles forced abandonment of the scheme.

In fact, Castle Leslie's proximity to the border and the increasing sectarian violence occurring in Northern Ireland put paid to any hopes of tourism development in the region for the next three decades. By September 1973 Desmond had to inform Larry Mott, an American cousin, that

> the hotel scheme is dead. But perhaps it is a blessing in disguise. It may have been too big and ruined the magic ambiance of Glaslough … a huge hotel disgorging coachloads of blue rinse ladies 'doing' Europe, complaining about the air conditioning, the central heating and the fact that Irish food actually tastes like food and not like processed garbage.

It was typical of Desmond that in public he would always try to put a positive spin even on the worst circumstances.

N I N E

AFTER FIVE YEARS of failing to make money from the Castle Leslie estate, indeed of watching it drain his already meagre financial
resources, Desmond was under tremendous strain not least because
his personal life remained as tumultuous as ever. For some time even
before moving back to Ireland he had been deeply involved with the
woman who would become his second wife. Ten years Desmond's
junior and the daughter of a British army colonel, Helen Strong was
raised in a small Somerset village until the outbreak of the Second
World War when she went to stay in Herefordshire with a wealthy
spinster aunt, Violet Dowden. Only at the age of fourteen did she
begin to receive any formal education, after which she trained as a
teacher and worked for a period at a primary school. But soon she
moved to Gibraltar where, Desmond once wrote, she was popularly
known as 'wits and something that rhymes with it'. There she made

Helen on the ski slopes, 1970s.

money by smuggling whisky on a speedboat across the Spanish border, eventually crossing it herself to live in Torremolinos, at the time a small fishing village. Here it was possible to live comfortably on very little money, especially after Violet Dowden died and left Helen a legacy from which she was able to draw a modest income. This she supplemented by intermittently running a florist business whenever in London.

In the winter of 1958 she was in the Austrian ski resort of Kitzbuhl, staying with retired Vice-Admiral Philip Ruck-Keene who had commanded the aircraft-carrier HMS *Formidable* during the later stages of the war. One afternoon she and Desmond met for the first time; he was staying in the same resort, not with Agnes but with his current girlfriend. Before guests arrived for tea, Ruck-Keene warned Helen that among their number would be a fascinating man she ought to avoid because he already had 'a 100 volt wife and an exotic mistress – so you're allowed just to look'. On that occasion, Helen 'slid into the room in a rather tight sweater. Then I looked and looked, but nothing happened.' Nevertheless, when next in London she was invited to a party by Desmond, who had taken the trouble while in Kitzbuhl to secure her address. He subsequently suggested the pair of them have lunch, which they did in a hotel, with a room upstairs previously booked by Desmond. At the end of the meal, the two of them took advantage of its facilities.

Almost six foot tall, with long blonde hair and a voluptuous figure, Helen Strong made an immediate and irrevocable impression on Desmond – whom she named 'The Over-Sexed Perambulating Encyclopaedia'. Her attraction to him was not just physical. 'Emotionally and psychically Helen and I were as one from the word go,' he told his elder son Sean in August 1968.

> I have never before felt that *belonging* to anyone except her ...
> I know it sounds silly and weak to you to say there are stronger
> forces than ourselves. But the fact is it is true. If I'd let her go

out of my life something would have died in me and gone very sad and grey and useless. We don't understand these torrential forces. It's like swimming in a stormy sea.

Just over a year later, he described Helen as 'the one and only woman in my life with whom every minute, every second is precious and without whom we are only half-people.' And to his sister Anita he wrote that since meeting Helen, 'I have not looked at another woman with any desire to take her. When you are really happy with one person, you just don't want anything else. That, I believe, is the true meaning of fidelity.'

In *The Fun Palace*, Agnes conveys the impression that Helen was a friend of both herself and Desmond, and 'had somehow become an integral part of our lives'. Helen, on the other hand, disputes this notion, saying she and Agnes were never friendly. But Agnes was certainly aware of Helen's role in her husband's life; after all from the earliest days of their marriage she had witnessed Desmond run after many other women, most of whom were perfectly happy to be caught by him. According to their son Mark, when confronted with evidence of the relationship between Helen and Desmond, Agnes said, 'Of course, I knew. That's fine, I'm not shocked. My father was a very happily married man but he had mistresses, my brother too. There are very few interesting or intelligent men that I know that haven't at some stage been unfaithful to their wives.' Only the naive, she implied, allowed themselves to be upset by marital infidelity. Helen was close enough to the couple to help with the organization of a party marking Desmond's fortieth birthday in June 1961.

Held in a private garden in Chelsea, the occasion was meant to evoke a Roman orgy, with tiger skins spread on the lawn, bunches of grapes hung from tree branches overhead, a stuffed lion in the coal cellar and a large notice declaring 'Christians This Way'. Guests arrived wearing sheets and bedspreads as imitation togas, and with wreaths in their hair. All went well until someone leaned against an unstable pillar, which toppled over and spilt the contents of a bowl of burning methylated spirits on to the tiger skins. These burst into flames, one of the guests hurt himself attempting to extinguish the fire in bare feet and the fire brigade and ambulance services were called, with journalists swarming in their wake. The following day's newspapers carried headlines such as 'Rome Burns in SW7' and Desmond quoted saying, 'Ah yes, we burn Christians in Chelsea.'

When Desmond moved to Castle Leslie in the winter of 1963, Helen Strong came too. But this arrangement ended once Agnes and the new baby finally arrived in Ireland the following spring and settled into the family home. Later that year, Desmond and Helen decided to separate and she went to stay with friends, Connie and Jimmy Wilson, in the Bahamian resort of Nassau, where she became an extra on the James Bond film *Thunderball*. Before long Desmond was thoroughly miserable and unable to bear their separation. In early March 1965 he wrote to Helen,

> Darling, Darling Love, I cannot live without you. There is no joy, no nothing. I have been in abject darkness since September when you went away from here, and the darkness is increasing … You must be exposed to all sorts of delightful temptations. Darling, enjoy yourself, but please please please don't start to get 'involved'. If you feel yourself being dangerously drawn away from me please come home. I know it seems a lot to ask you when you are having such a lovely time, but if I lost you now we might never be together again.

Unable to survive without at least hearing Helen's voice, Desmond drove up to Belfast, booked himself into a hotel and telephoned Nassau. The next day he wrote to her, 'I have reached the age when one truly loves. At my age one does not change again. I know I shall *never* not love you … There is only one thing I require – to be with you. I have never loved anyone like you and will never love anyone else like you.' Despite his earlier record with women, this actually proved to be the case. Twenty years later, Desmond could declare, 'It's really terribly hard for me to be without Helen for more than a few days … I'm like one of those people on a kidney machine. I'm on a Helen machine and need her constantly, or I start to wilt and the joy in my life dies.' Eventually Helen returned from the Bahamas and moved into a flat in a large Victorian house in the Dublin suburb of Terenure where Desmond often stayed with her. 'I went ahead to find somewhere to live,' she remembered. 'The area seemed quite nice, a huge house divided into eight different apartments, one for us, one for the nanny.' The latter was necessary because at the beginning of 1966 Helen became pregnant and that September gave birth in a private nursing home in Hatch Street, Dublin, to her first child, Samantha, always known as Sammy; at the time Desmond was in County Monaghan.

By this date his marriage to Agnes had broken down irrevo-cably although the two of them continued to live under the same roof; understandably she had no desire to move out of Castle Leslie. After all, at Desmond's insistence she had given up her life and career in London and moved to Ireland. Unable to find work as an actress, she pursued the idea of a clothing business in Mona-ghan and started a small knitwear company called Castle Shane. But because he wanted to live openly and constantly with Helen, Desmond tried various means to encourage Agnes's departure from Castle Leslie – without success. He argued that their marriage had been a mistake, informing his son Sean,

> I don't think Agi is my twin soul. I think she is more of a twin sister, and as such we could have a splendid relationship …
> It was her mind and companionship I most enjoyed, and still could enjoy. Had I my life over again, I wouldn't have rushed into an early marriage. But I was high and dry and lonely at the end of the war and felt I had no real home. Cancer people are great home lovers and I wanted a home very much. One lives and learns …

Desmond and Helen with Sammy at the latter's christening, 1966.

Likewise he told his sister Anita,

> While Agnes might have been right for me 20 years ago our
> chemistries simply do not harmonise. She has tried her best and
> I hold her no grudge nor ill-will. But you cannot force the impos-
> sible. Sooner or later I was bound to have to face this truth, and
> to have it forced upon me by coming face to face with the person
> who is right for me and whose mere presence can give me greater
> happiness and tranquillity than any other human being.

By now, anyone who knew Desmond was aware of his predicament, not least because he discussed it with all his friends. 'I think to hope to amalgamate the two families could be asking too much,' wrote Grace Cooke, a woman he often consulted during these years. 'But if you can come to a working arrangement with Agnes while she is established at Glaslough and Helen could live her own life (it would mean running two homes of course) I do think this could be the solution.' As word of what was going on became widespread, Anita desperately tried to stem the gossip by writing to her beleaguered sister-in-law,

> I did not mean to criticise when I said 'Be Discreet' – I only meant it in the same way you shout to a person drowning in a river when you are on the bank and it looks easy to say 'Keep Calm – Don't Lose Your Head – Swim With the Current' etc. Let us all try to remain as reticent and dignified (Don't laugh at old-fashioned word!) as possible.

Desmond's inability to find a satisfactory resolution to his unusual circumstances dragged on for the next couple of years, with Agnes resolutely in Castle Leslie and Helen in Dublin. 'How do you think you can improve on this situation?' Anita asked her brother in September 1968. 'You see *everyone* is appalled at the general unhappiness & every friend as well as every member of the family would love to see you and Agnes and Helen and all the children happier. No one is against you – we only want to help straighten out in your own mind the steps you are going to take.' As Desmond and Agnes's daughter Antonia would later remember, 'There was awful friction in those years. My mother didn't want to let go, and he wasn't knowing which way to turn and which one to be with and it all got nastier and nastier.'

A year later – by which time he and Helen had a second daughter, Camilla, born at Dublin's Rotunda Hospital in March 1969 – Desmond finally took a decisive step.

I am too old to go on wasting my life, it is too short [he informed Helen]. If I throw away this chance, I shall end up a bitter old man, devoid of love, kindness and any kind of spirituality. If I give in to it I shall have more love than I deserve and may have a number of personal problems regarding my family. But I must face them. I cannot live without you – therefore I must have you ALWAYS.

In late summer 1969 he persuaded Agnes to take their two younger children Mark and Antonia on holiday to Yugoslavia and Venice. When the trio returned to Castle Leslie one evening in August, it was to find the house locks had all been changed, leaving them unable to enter what had until then been the family home. 'I remember my mother going up to put the key in the lock and it was changed,' Antonia later recalled; at the time of this incident she was not yet six. Unable to gain admission through the main entrance, Agnes

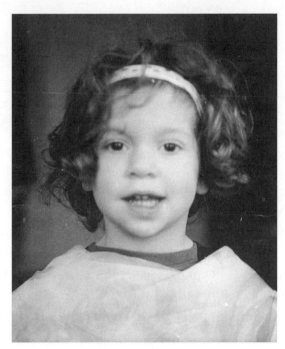

Antonia as a little girl, 1960s.

went round to the side and it was locked so she rang the door bell and I remember Dad coming to the door with a guy called Larry Mott and being very nice and standing in the door and saying, 'Hi, how are you? How was your holiday? I don't know why you have these suitcases because you don't live here anymore.'

Agnes and Antonia being turned away from Castle Leslie, 1969, with Larry Mott.

Larry Mott was one of Desmond's American cousins with whom he had established contact and who would later become involved with the abortive scheme to develop a golf course on the estate. In the summer of 1969 he and his wife Fran were visiting Ireland and Desmond persuaded him to assume temporary ownership of Castle Leslie, thereby stripping Agnes of her right to live in the house. That evening she and the two children found themselves homeless with no possessions other than the clothes they had been wearing while on holiday. After a brief stay at Oranmore Castle with Desmond's sister Anita, Agnes and the children returned to Glaslough where the local residents heard of their predicament and rallied round; they were able to stay temporarily in the local hotel, after which accommodation was found for them in the village by Monaghan County Council.

Though his children later forgave him, it is hard to excuse Desmond's behaviour. In late November 1969 he wrote to a friend,

> my first three children have elected to disown me and go with their mother Agnes. But I think they will come back to me one day when they realise that for this heritage to be preserved, there had to be a showdown, and agonising though it was, I had to appear cruel to my dearest ones so they could one day enjoy their heritage. They don't understand the 'whys' at the moment … Darling Helen is in France with her children, and it seems must stay away from me until all tangles are sorted out. So those dear children are also out of my life at the moment.

It was surely disingenuous of Desmond to argue his behaviour had been motivated by a wish for 'this heritage' to be preserved since his marital status was irrelevant to the estate's future. The facts are that he no longer wished to live with Agnes and wanted instead to live with Helen. Agnes refused to concede to his wishes or even to leave Castle Leslie. Since she would not go into voluntary exile, he forced banishment on her and, as a consequence, on the couple's children. It would take a long time for the damage he caused by his actions to be repaired. On the other hand, in his defence Desmond was clearly under so much pressure he could not be considered entirely responsible for his behaviour. The demands of trying to hold on to Castle Leslie were enormous and Mark remembers his father at the time going through terrible mood swings, often losing his temper and slamming doors or shutting himself off from his family.

Desmond and Helen at the races, mid-1970s.

Desmond was conscious of the hurt he had caused his children, later asking Mark:

> Try and forgive me for not being as good a father to you as I should be. But as I've often tried to say to you, getting my own life in a bit of a muddle doesn't make me love you any less. In fact it makes me love you more. I hope you'll be able to understand that one day and will have a less turbulent existence than me.

It wasn't only his offspring who found Desmond difficult to deal with during this period. Apologizing for his behaviour to Anita, he explained, 'If I sometimes appear silent and withdrawn it is because I am turning things over in my head regarding the management here. Of course my personal problems have not helped, and they couldn't have come at a worse time.' A younger man might have coped better but Desmond was now in his mid-forties and neither emotionally nor physically able to cope with the strain. The combined financial and personal problems took a serious toll, as he admitted to Mark a few years later. 'I was in a state of suspended nervous breakdown,' he wrote.

> I couldn't let myself go completely and have a mental collapse as I felt that if I did the whole thing would fall apart. So we just kept on doggedly coping from day to day, and working out schemes until the right one turned up ... What was doubly unfortunate is that the financial crisis and the personal crisis should come on top of one another, and it is only by the Grace of God we have survived this far ... Communicating when in a state of acute stress is terribly difficult, and I must have seemed very withdrawn and grey at times – for which I'm sorry as it must have distressed you.

In order to cope, Desmond resorted to taking prescribed medication, often in excessive dosages. Anita observed on at least one visit to Castle Leslie that 'I found Desmond very hard to talk to – he did not concentrate or follow any line of thought for 5 minutes – I gathered he was heavily dosed with tranquilisers. My heart sank as for the first time I felt it impossible for Glaslough to survive under such management.' In other words, when Desmond arranged for the locks of Castle Leslie to be changed and Agnes denied entrance, he was unlikely to have been thinking rationally. Had he done so, he would have understood the likely and dreadful consequences of his behaviour.

In any case, full awareness of what he had done was not long coming. Within a year, he was writing of a 'desperate longing for spiritual absolution and forgiveness for the hurt I did to my children and Agi … Until my children have come back – if ever – and say they forgive me, my soul will remain heavily burdened.' Around the same time, he wrote to Mark's headmaster at Ampleforth: 'It's terribly hard for children to understand adult problems, nor should they be put in a position where they have to try and do so.' By then Desmond had had no contact with Mark for over a year and wanted to visit the school in the hope of a rapprochement with his younger son. 'We may not be successful but at least we can have a try. Mark's a wonderful boy and I miss him very much.'

Rapprochement would follow, not just with Mark but with the other children too, although it was not easy, particularly for Antonia. She only met her half-sister Sammy when the two of them were attending the same school in Glaslough – some time after Agnes's departure from Castle Leslie, Helen and her two daughters came to live there permanently.

Sammy and Antonia quickly bonded and after seeing where the latter lived, Sammy suggested they go to play in her house; Antonia found herself in what had previously been her bedroom looking at what had been her toys. Though the local authority provided Agnes with somewhere to live in the village, she and Antonia spent much of their time in Dublin where they shared a house in Booterstown with Joanne Clements and her six children; Joanne's husband Marcus, also struggling to maintain a historic family estate, had similarly

Helen with Sammy at Castle Leslie.

left her for another woman. Ironically, from Agnes's perspective, the house was on a street called St Helen's Road. To make some money, she and Joanne opened a clothes shop called Ambush in an arcade off Grafton Street in central Dublin.

But despite the rancour, Agnes and Desmond had to stay in touch if only because he provided the money to support their children. In early December 1970, he wrote to her,

> A little money – a soupçon – has most timely arrived from America, so before it all gets lost paying dreary things like bills here is £200 for the family Christmas … I thought I'd send it now so as to give you time to plan something nice for the children. You don't have to tell them I've sent it unless you want to. Get yourself something nice out of it as well if poss.

He and Agnes then started to correspond regularly, she pretending it was Antonia who had written her letters and he conniving in this expedient deception. On Ambush notepaper Antonia/Agnes wrote to Desmond in early 1971 informing him that 'Mummy says you might really let us have a home now and then Sammy and I could at least go and stay with each other and I could have my own little room where I could keep my things safe from four-year-old fingers!!! Please dear Daddy, do it soon.'

He replied on a sheet of paper headed 'Nonswinging Gear for Squares and Elderly Daddies' and giving the impression that Sammy was responsible for the first paragraph: 'This is Sami speekin. Mie splelign iz knot verry gud as I amm ownlee a chield progedy of for yers auld an am ownlee afluent in for lingages – Inglich, Urdu, Sanskrit an Dorric. Soe I wil git Dady to right the wrest.' In March 1971 he asked Antonia,

> Please tell Mummy I am so glad we had such a nice talk and that I fully agree with the principles of the document I showed her. The idea is ... that she looks round for a house that would really suit you all and prove a good investment for you. We may have to hock the jewels as a temporary measure as all my sales and deals have been hopelessly slow ... I just don't know what has happened to my Stars. Every damn way I move to try and get Glaslough solvent and cash for the family seems to bog down, go slow, and give me ulcers (or try to).

As they negotiated a legal settlement that would include the provision of a home in Dublin for Agnes, her correspondence with Desmond even managed to be occasionally jokey, with their respective solicitors nicknamed 'Mucky Hands' and 'McAnnulment'. 'Tell Mummy to ask McAnnulment for some information regarding his talks,' Desmond wrote to Antonia. 'And for God's sake, don't let him horse things up any more. This "taking of attitudes" may be very fine and mighty, but it's his poor client who suffers for it.'

Not long afterwards, Agnes told 'Dear Daddy' that

Mummy has phoned McAnnulment's office and was told that 'the documents' were sent off to Mucky Hands for approval and comment and have not so far been returned … If you want quick action and especially if you want me [namely Antonia] to come and stay officially (and it can only be officially as too many people would know about it), please get Mucky Hands to get a move on. We will hurry McAnnulment from our end.

Agnes had found a house on Strand Road in Dublin and after several months scrambling around for money – including the use of his mother's jewels as security for the bank – Desmond eventually managed to raise the necessary funds to buy it for her. 'This letter,' he informed Agnes in early May 1971, 'is my irrevocable instruction to proceed with the purchase of the house, whether I should die, be committed to a nuthouse, or abducted by an UFO. It is therefore a binding commitment.'

By now Agnes had met architectural historian Maurice Craig with whom she would spend the rest of her life. In November 1971 Desmond wrote to a friend in England that he and Agnes were 'friendly again, and I have managed to borrow money to buy her the house she wants in Dublin (more bloody debts!). But I really wanted to do this to make up to her for so much that went wrong. She is coming up this weekend with Maurice to her cottage in the village and Antonia is coming here. Agi and Helen have not met again yet, nor do I expect them to want to do so for quite a long time.' And yet, just three months later, he was able to announce, 'Helen took all the children and all their village friends to the Panto in Dublin and yesterday had tea with Agi! I can't wait to hear a full report …' In January 1973, he declared himself

slightly exhausted as we have had a day-long, but very friendly, meeting with Helen, Agnes and Maurice, merely trying to sort out our host of material worries and complications – but it was very amiable and constructive … who would have thought, two or three years ago, that we four would have sat down together in such a good frame of mind.

Thereafter, with intermittent hiccups, relations between Desmond and Agnes were good. He and Helen sometimes stayed in the Strand Road house when they visited Dublin and this hospitality was reciprocated in Castle Leslie. At least one aspect of Desmond's life began to show signs of stability.

Helen and Agnes at Castle Leslie, c.1962–3.
Left to right: Richard Harries Jones, Agnes, Sean, Helen.

TEN

ADDING TO THE emotional turbulence of this period, Desmond lost his father when Sir Shane Leslie died in August 1971. Although living in England for many years with his second wife Iris, he had returned every year to Castle Leslie, usually spending a month or two in the house in the early autumn. In August 1965, just a few weeks before the annual visit that would coincide with his eightieth birthday, he loftily instructed Desmond, 'I want no celebration but prepare all the schools on the old estate for a school feast – Catholic and Protestant – for which I will pay.'

In his final years, he was inclined to reminisce about the past and about the changes that had occurred during his lifetime, not always – to his way of thinking – for the better. 'If I had not been so old, I would have grieved when the books and trees were removed wholesale,' he told Desmond in June 1968, lamenting the need

View of Castle Leslie.

for sales to raise money for an estate over which he had never had authority. But the following year he was able to congratulate his son on holding on to the family home: 'It will be possible that the old place will continue.' After his death, Shane's widow retained the habit of visiting Castle Leslie every year. So too did Desmond's brother Jack who would travel from Italy to spend several weeks in Ireland, usually during the month of August. And even though she had handed it over to Desmond in 1963, Anita continued to be attached to the estate and concerned for its well-being.

As, indeed, she had good reason to be because Desmond's financial problems remained as acute as ever. If anything, the departure of Agnes aggravated his circumstances; on top of all the other demands, now he had to find money to support her in Dublin as well. In December 1970 he assured Agnes that he had paid Mark's school fees for Ampleforth but even six years later, by which time Mark had left not only school but also university, a monk in the Procurator's office at Ampleforth was pressing Desmond for final payment, apologizing for 'having to bother you with this but we, like everyone else, suffer from a cash flow problem and I have had to take urgent steps to call in all outstanding debts … I look forward to receiving your cheque as soon as you can.'

In order to come up with enough money for the purchase of Agnes's house on Strand Road, Desmond decided to sell one of the last valuable paintings from what had, less than a century before, been among the country's finest private art collection. This was the *Flight into Egypt* by sixteenth-century north-Italian artist Jacopo Bassano; brought to Ireland by Desmond's great-grandfather, the first Sir John Leslie, it had ever since hung over the drawing-room fireplace.

But in the summer of 1971, around the time of his father's death, Desmond decided to include the picture in an old masters sale at Christie's. 'We hope it makes enough to set up Agi with the nice house we are trying to buy her and a bit more income,' he told an English friend. The picture did sell, but Desmond felt its loss, telling Jack that when the Bassano left Castle Leslie, 'I shed a few tears … It was like a death in the family.' From Rome Jack proposed that he commission a perfect copy of both the painting and its carved and gilded frame. Desmond was thrilled with the idea. 'It will be really wonderful having the picture back again,' he told his brother. 'The drawing room hasn't been the same without it. That marvellous gleam from the ornate frame and the lovely grouping of the figures really was the essence of the room. I can't tell you how grateful I am to you for it!' Just before the Bassano copy arrived at Castle Leslie, he told Jack, 'We cannot wait to see it hanging proudly on the wall again … It really will be the most exciting moment when it is rehung in the drawing room. I've never wanted to go into that room since it went to the salesroom.'

The Bassano was not the last item to go: there were to be other sales over the years ahead, and not just of artworks from the house. Already in 1970 Desmond had disposed of some 340 acres of the estate to a Northern Irish businessman, Desmond Mallon, because, as he wrote to Joan Hodgson in England that November,

> the wolves close in on the physical plane and I've had, at last, to sell off some strips of land which is heart-breaking … Everything I've attempted business wise seems to have gone wrong – signed contracts in hand, written guarantees, promises, undertakings – all welshed on time and time again; making me begin to wonder and question the purpose of going on, or to question whether I was on the right track.

The following year, the obligation to repay extended bank loans forced him to offer Mallon the Castle Leslie farm. Hearing of this, Anita and Bill offered to buy it instead. They did so and transferred the farm to their son Tarka's name. Anita would also purchase outright a parcel of land immediately beside the house and a large lakeside field known as Killyconigan. Though these sales temporarily brought him financial relief, Desmond did not relish letting go of any part of the estate, and especially not to his sister. 'I'm the one who has to worry,' he snapped at her during negotiations over the farm sale. 'I, with the whole bloody burden of rates and upkeep and no estate portfolio from which to pay them. If I had no more financial worries than the sum of yours and Jack's added together, I should sleep easy at night.'

After Tarka King began spending time on the farm from 1977 onwards, he and Desmond maintained a distinctly combative relationship, writing to each other as 'Usurping Nephew' and 'Wicked Uncle'. It was obviously not easy for the older man to see someone younger take over land that had once been in his possession, and to make a success of it. On the other hand, Desmond's constant need for cash meant that during the next twenty years additional sections of the estate, along with a number of outlying buildings such as gate lodges, would also have to be sold. (One of them, Dawson's Lodge, was bought by his brother Jack.)

But he pressed on with various schemes, confident a means would yet be discovered to make Castle Leslie financially viable. Though the plans for a hotel and for a golf resort had both failed to progress, Desmond was sure the estate could be developed as a tourist attraction, albeit with a specific market in mind. In March 1971, under the guise of writing to Antonia, he told Agnes that,

> As all writers are now tax-free, I'm seriously going about long-leasing lodges, or building sites … to high income English artists; one might raise quite substantial sums very quickly by so doing. I have found up to 12 sites which would not in the least spoil the demesne if done tastefully out of rough stone, timber, etc harmonising with the site … don't spread this around. You could, however, keep an ear to the ground for sound of high income artists looking for a retreat in Ireland.

But if artists were looking for an Irish retreat, it wouldn't be at Castle Leslie because when theatre director Tyrone Guthrie died in May 1971 he bequeathed his own County Monaghan family home, Annamakerrig, to the Irish State to be developed for this very purpose. In the meantime, Desmond had moved on to other possibilities, such as a notion he outlined in early 1972 to Dr Tim O'Driscoll, newly retired Director General of the Irish Tourist Board, for Castle Leslie to be turned into a 'wildlife sanctuary and conservation research centre … The point is of course that Glaslough is absolutely unpolluted, uncontaminated and ecologically still untarnished, so it would be an ideal place to set up such a trust.'

Two years later, he had come up with yet another plan, this one being that he hand over full management and control of Castle Leslie to an American businessman called Jay Colwell. In August, the two men signed an agreement whereby, as Desmond explained, Colwell would 'take over all my debts, and commitments, take over the ownership and the running and the outlays on the whole estate on a business arrangement. He will also pay me quite a handy sum each year for the next twenty years. From a strict business viewpoint it looks silly both from his end and from mine.' At this remove, the proposal still looks silly and quickly ran into trouble, but only after Desmond had received – and spent – an advance of $25,000. It's difficult to know quite what were Jay Colwell's intentions, other than to gain control of an Irish property the owner of which was seriously strapped for cash. Within a year Desmond was writing to an English friend,

> It is hard to know quite what is going on. I think J.C. was genuine when he first came here but it looks terribly as if it developed into a risky con trick to unseat me and take over … Such a shame as I do believe he once had the right intentions but that when he found things too difficult he resorted to misrepresentation, hoping things would turn out alright in the end … Documents have been signed, but my lawyers think they can be invalidated.

They could and in 1976 Colwell and Desmond came to a new arrangement whereby the former relinquished any rights he had to Castle Leslie as soon as the money he had advanced was returned. The problem was that this money had long since been used up and more besides borrowed from two banks on the strength of the initial contract. Desmond now had to find funds in a hurry and was only saved on this occasion by his brother Jack who raised the necessary cash by disposing of property he owned in Rome.

As if this scenario were not sufficiently muddled, it transpired that Desmond had been in separate but simultaneous discussions with two different government departments about the possibility of the State assuming responsibility for the estate. In June 1976 he confessed,

> A few weeks ago I was terribly worried that I'd made yet another mess. I'm still not sure. It was like this – way back in 1972 I wrote to the Forestry Department and asked if they'd like to buy and manage about 250 acres of young woodland to save me rates and wages. Eventually they agreed. Their letter agreeing came the day I'd signed the contract in 1974 with our American and not-lamented Jay Colwell. Luckily I did not decline their offer. I merely ignored it, and was incredibly vague when they eventually rang to ask what was happening. But earlier in 1974 we had asked the National Parks Department if they'd like to take over most of the estate and make it into a beautiful nature reserve and public park.

Once the Colwell scheme came to an end, Desmond reverted first to the Parks Department, which appeared interested in 'total preservation by the State for all time, taking the whole big load off me, leaving me with just the house and garden'. But then each organization learnt of the other's negotiations with Castle Leslie and Desmond realized that he had 'dropped another monumental clanger by trying to deal with two departments at once'. The Parks Department pulled out altogether while the Forestry Department pursued its interest in purchasing the woodland for commercial development and even signed a contract to do so. At which point Tarka King, who had only recently come to live on the farm acquired by his parents six years before, heard what was taking place and offered to buy the woodland himself, eventually doing so in January 1978.

These misadventures cruelly exposed Desmond's want of entre-preneurial acumen. He had no training, either in business or farm-ing, and managing the estate during those difficult years demanded skills he simply did not possess in sufficient quantity. On the other hand, his commitment to Castle Leslie cannot be questioned. 'You see, dear Jack,' he wrote to his brother in January 1973, 'I have suf-fered the continual nightmare in the last ten years of trying to run this estate on my little American income plus what I could try to make from the farm. The continued and unrelenting worry has greatly strained my health and I am just not capable of carrying on much longer.'

But he did carry on, and for considerably longer, because he felt obliged to do so, obliged to find some means of keeping Cas-tle Leslie within the family. Lack of funds meant he and Helen could not pay staff and had to do much of the estate work them-selves. 'Helen marvellously runs the four acre walled garden and greenhouses,' he wrote in June 1976, 'with one man and her own planning and manages the house superbly. How, I don't know. She is exhausted at the end of each day.' A year later, Desmond wrote to Jack that 'We've had 3 tons of apples and sold a lot to the mar-kets. Will live on and deep-freeze the rest as stew, ditto spuds. Since Helen took over the garden, we practically live off the land.' Build-ing an equestrian course on the estate in spring 1975, Desmond was on site every day. 'The weather has been the wettest in all memory,' he told his brother, 'so that our earth-moving and ditch digging machinery has foundered in swamps and we've had to move soil, gravel and stones literally by hand, like Maoist coolies building the "Comrades' Dam". Only trouble is that there were only four of us instead of several million.'

View of Castle Leslie.

Desmond often found himself frustrated by dealing with government authorities and their demands on his time. Pestered for documentation on the dissolved Sir John Leslie Estate Company, Desmond advised the relevant civil servant that the person who could best advise on this matter was a Monaghan solicitor who had acted as company secretary but had since died. 'It seems therefore that we must contact the late Robert Brett for the information you require,' he wrote in February 1976. 'I am shortly seeing a very good medium. Would you like me to try and contact the late departed and see what information he can supply?' Likewise in August 1977, Desmond congratulated the secretary of Monaghan County Council on a new fence and gates the local authority had installed around the Glaslough sewage works that stood on land once part of the estate.

> I should like to point out that the workmen have put the concrete fence poles with the sloping top facing inwards rather than outwards, and I hope that when the fence is continued they won't make the same mistake. The idea was, of course, to keep vandals out rather than to keep the Leslies in. It has been suggested by the uncharitable that the Leslies should be locked up!

Many of the problems Desmond faced during these years were not specific to him but typical of those that caused other owners of historic Irish estates to abandon homes that had been in the possession of their families for centuries. While a certain number of important houses were burnt down during the early 1920s – including nearby Castle Shane, whose occupants the Scudamores afterwards took refuge with the Leslies – far more were either pulled down or allowed to fall into ruin during the middle decades of the twentieth century. Ireland at that time was an extremely poor country, with little money to spend on preserving the national heritage. But nor was there much interest in doing so, even after the establishment of the

Irish Georgian Society by the Hon. Desmond and Mariga Guinness in 1958. The fate of the 'Big House' was a subject of widespread indifference and many distinguished old properties in Monaghan such as Dartry and Rossmore Park, both of which Desmond would have known well as a young man, were demolished without any protest. Estates in Northern Ireland could be handed over into the care of the British National Trust but no such organization existed in the South where owners were expected to look after their properties and not seek State support. They struggled to survive, like Desmond, by selling off outlying parts of an estate or disposing of valuable furniture and works of art within the house.

The difficulties faced by Castle Leslie were compounded by its location, with a long stretch of the estate wall marking the border between the Northern and Southern jurisdictions. Smugglers seeking to evade the police and customs authorities often took a short cut across Desmond's fields, but this behaviour was relatively harmless when compared with what happened once the 'Troubles' broke out in the late 1960s. Bombings, shootings and other acts of violence quickly became the norm, peaking in 1972 when more than 450 people in Northern Ireland lost their lives; the mortality figures were not much better for the rest of the decade and beyond. Whatever hopes Desmond may have entertained about opening Castle Leslie as an hotel, country club or golf course, or establishing the estate as a tourist destination, these were quickly scuppered once sectarian violence became rife across the border. Besides anything else, it was no longer possible to guarantee the safety of guests. Many members of the Provisional Irish Republican Army lived in the Republic and travelled north under cover of darkness or across land such as the Castle Leslie estate, which could not be patrolled by the security forces. Desmond would remember on one occasion meeting 'a well-known provo avoiding road blocks by taking a handy short-cut round the lake. He had just blown up the post office at Middletown and was carrying a fishing rod as disguise – the only odd thing about the rod was that the line had no hook!'

More seriously, on another occasion the Provisional IRA attempted to kidnap a man then staying at Castle Leslie on an equestrian holiday under the mistaken belief that he was a member of the British security forces. When Desmond intervened, one of the would-be kidnappers drew a gun and pointed it directly at him. 'What really bugged me,' Desmond later dryly remarked, 'was that he had the cheek to do this inside my front gates, which I felt was exceptionally bad form.' What had once been a rather sleepy border area grew steadily more volatile, with the threat of imminent lawlessness always present. Fortunately, certain features of local life remained the same. In January 1973 Desmond told his brother of a 'lovely announcement after Christmas mass by Father McCarney: "There may be a Mass at Coracrin this week, or there may not be. It all depends if I'm sober or not." End of announcement. Then, as an afterthought: "If you see me around, there probably will be." Some things, fortunately, have not changed.'

But in the face of escalating lawlessness, it became steadily harder to maintain a cheerful disposition. Letters Desmond wrote to Grace Cooke and her daughter Joan Hodgson in England show how dispirited he grew as a result of the violence which, he felt, 'has just become a way of life, like the weather, and short of plague, pestilence or cataclysm, no end is in sight. Ireland has the most marvellous talent for missing the boat, missing its chances and buggering things up.' As early as March 1971 he was commenting, 'We just don't know what is going to happen any more. The blind hatreds and fears have got out of control in Belfast and the dark brothers are having a field day whispering in every inflamed ear. We feel so helpless against this cloud of culpable darkness.' Nine months later he wrote, 'Either reconciliation must come *soon* or the country will go berserk. For every outrage further separates the communities and adds to the terrible cloud of hatred which, short of divine intervention, is going to take so long to disperse.'

It did take a long time; ten years on, Desmond was writing in the same vein to Joan Hodgson, saying he now believed the violence

> isn't likely to end in my lifetime … Of only one thing can you be sure in this tragic beautiful bitch of a country – that what can be screwed up will be screwed up. The dreadful thing is that I can see both sides, and feel desperately sorry for all of them. Sorry for the old guard for being such blind arrogant fools for so long, sorry for the people for what they had to, and still have to, put up with. Sorry that this, one of the loveliest unspoilt countries in Europe has to have the joy knocked out of its everyday life when just a little good will and a little good luck at the right moments could have solved so much.

Although neither Desmond and his family nor Castle Leslie ever directly suffered attacks during this unhappy period, there were plenty of occasions when the impact of the Troubles was felt close to home. In January 1973 the Provisional IRA detonated a bomb at Caledon, badly damaging the home of one of Desmond's nearest neighbours, a family closely connected with his own for almost two hundred years. 'I immediately went over with a sympathy note from us all,' he told Jack, describing the bomb as 'a particularly beastly experience' for the Earl of Caledon since he 'had only just completed two years' extensive restoration on the house and he was very depressed about it all'.

Much more tragically, in January 1981 another immediate neighbour, former Speaker of the Northern Ireland House of Commons Sir Norman Stronge and his only son James were killed by the Provisional IRA in their family home, Tynan Abbey, which was then burnt to the ground. The perpetrators were believed to have escaped by fleeing across the adjacent Castle Leslie estate. 'It's a great shock and outrage to have such a vile attack perpetrated on the people just next door,' he exclaimed to Joan Hodgson a few days later.

Subsequently he wrote to Jack in Rome that the Stronges had been given a 'huge funeral, to which we all went. I sent a big wreath, "To our much loved and respected friends and neighbours from the Leslie family" which I felt covered us all. Good showing from the south … but a cold rage among everyone including us I can tell you.' It was the seeming endlessness of attack and counter-attack by the two opposing sides that Desmond found so depressing. 'I only feel sad at the needless suffering going on,' he informed Joan Hodgson, and at

> the endlessly missed opportunities. Again and again the time has been right for a settlement, and time and again either through ill fortune, some silly mistake or plain bloody cussedness, the chance has slipped and gone forever … I suppose the trouble will resolve itself one day; it's been going on for the last 800 years with the present participants. It's just about time they forgave and packed it in.

Desmond tried to find ways to help. In the early years of the Troubles, he arranged for groups of children from the west Belfast district of Ballymurphy to come to Castle Leslie on camping holidays, but this had to be discontinued after threats were received from Loyalist groups. And in December 1971 he offered the Ardoyne Housing Committee a large quantity of wood from the estate to help rebuild two hundred homes destroyed by bombing.

Somehow he managed to hold on to his sense of humour even in the face of cross-border incursions by the British army. When large numbers of troops were first deployed in Northern Ireland, they often found it difficult to distinguish the boundary between the two jurisdictions. On one occasion Desmond found a group of squaddies dressed in camouflage preparing to brew tea on a primus stove set up on the lawn in front of the house; they had misread their map and believed themselves to be in the grounds of Caledon immediately across the border. The error explained, they were officially now classified as 'prisoners of war' and accordingly requested to come into Castle Leslie. While the men dried off their clothing, Desmond discovered the officer in charge had, like himself, attended Ampleforth. After tea, it was agreed the entire patrol should sign the house visitors' book as prisoners before being permitted to stage a mass break-out and escape back into Northern Ireland.

Less amusing were the times when a British army helicopter would land in the gardens so that its occupants could relieve themselves. After this had happened once too often, Desmond wrote an open postcard to General Sir Harry Tuzo, Commander of Operations in Northern Ireland for two years from 1971. Desmond proposed that the British army helicopters be equipped with either accurate maps or else Elsans since the existing scenario was undermining the hygiene of the Irish Republic. Tuzo replied in a similar vein with the assurance that in future airborne troops under his authority would only relieve themselves while hovering over Northern Irish territory. Desmond kept the general's card with him and was able to use it to his advantage when he and his son Mark were later stopped and harassed by a British army patrol in Belfast; seeing Tuzo's name, the troops immediately arranged for the Leslie car to be given an escort out of the area.

Not having the same family ties with Ireland, Helen found it harder to cope than did Desmond. 'Helen's gone skiing,' he told Joan Hodgson in February 1972. 'I sent her off as the vibes were getting her down. Difficult for a poonah colonel's daughter to tolerate or understand the Celtic cross currents of violence.' Eight years later he wrote to the same correspondent that Helen had 'got really fed up and went off to France with Camilla for a bit. I'm glad she's taken a break. This loony Celtic fog is too much for the

straight anglo-saxon-ancient-briton-roman. I'm more used to it.'
Desmond had also found an alternative source of emotional and
psychological support.

ELEVEN

AT SOME POINT in the 1950s Desmond came across a quasi-religious group in England, the White Eagle Lodge. He would be a fervent supporter of its activities for the rest of his life. 'You ask what is the White Eagle Lodge,' he wrote to Jack in March 1980 before going on to explain:

> The White Eagle is the symbol of St John (see Book of Kells and others) and we follow the special teaching given to St John regarding spiritual healing and cooperation with the Angelic Hierarchies. Our work is slow and unspectacular; we don't seek crowds nor publicity. As well as healing the sick, a major task is to dispel the spiritual fog and darkness that surrounds the planet as a result of all the fear and hatred and greed. In no way does it clash with 'orthodox' Christianity. Rather one could say it 'complements' it.

A non-profit making and non-proselytizing organization, the White Eagle Lodge was founded in London in 1936 by Grace Cooke. She had been working for a number of years as a spiritualist medium and in 1930 had been informed by a French group called the Fraternité des Polaires that the recently deceased Arthur Conan Doyle, author of the Sherlock Holmes novels and an ardent believer in spiritualism during his final years, had chosen her as the channel by which he wished to communicate from the other side.

Subsequently she was 'contacted' by a Native American spiritual guide called White Eagle – seemingly once a chief of one of the six tribes of the Iroquois – and founded the group named after him. As Grace Cooke explained, ' "White Eagle" is the name given to a personality who speaks through my instrumentality, using my brain and vocal organs to give his messages. It is not my voice because I could not speak as he does.' The White Eagle Lodge's core beliefs are that God is both Father and Mother, that human life is governed by five cosmic laws including reincarnation, that there is a connection between cause and effect, and that every experience in life is an opportunity for an individual to become more Godlike. Lodge membership is in three progressive stages: ordinary; 'outer brother'; and eventually 'inner brother'.

Desmond first heard about the White Eagle Lodge on a radio programme when still living in London and one day he and Agnes, who was suffering from intense migraine at the time, visited the group's London headquarters. As he began to introduce himself to Grace Cooke's daughter, Joan Hodgson, she interrupted to declare, 'We have been waiting for you for quite some time.' Both Desmond and Agnes returned many times afterwards and following their move to Ireland he began a regular correspondence with both Grace Cooke and Joan Hodgson.

One of the features of the White Eagle Lodge is that members are given names other than their own. Mrs Cooke, for example, was called 'Minesta' and her husband Ivan 'Faithful', while Desmond became 'Ahknaton' although this was often shortened to 'Aton', both names referring to the Pharaoh of the Eighteenth Dynasty of Egypt who died around 1336 BC. In 1973 Desmond was informed by the lodge, 'You are a bearer of light. In an incarnation in Egypt (as an ancient Egyptian) you are also very clearly linked with ourselves and you have a particular work to do for the Brotherhood.' Perhaps this was the same Egyptian who had appeared to Desmond many years before when he attended a séance conducted by Alec Harris in Cardiff?

From time to time, Desmond would receive messages directly from White Eagle, either during sessions he attended at one of the lodge's centres or via an intermediary. In March 1965, for example, Grace Cooke advised: 'White Eagle sends you his great love and assures you that all is known to him and the "Brothers" of the spirit side of life, and you have their understanding and their sympathy … The present crisis and pain in your heart will gradually diminish and we ask you to keep your true vision on your work.' As this message makes clear, the White Eagle Lodge provided Desmond with the kind of spiritual succour he had been seeking for a long time. Many of its core tenets also reflected his own beliefs and helped to give them a certain validity. But above all, the White Eagle Lodge offered Desmond uncritical support and encouragement; Grace Cooke, Joan Hodgson and other members of their circle never passed judgment on his behaviour or told him what he had done was wrong. Family, friends and acquaintances were often unsympathetically judgmental of Desmond's actions but not so the members of the White Eagle Lodge.

For more than forty years, they were unwavering in their gentle endorsement and in encouraging him to believe he had a duty to remain at Castle Leslie. 'Please do not apologise for coming to talk out your difficulties with me,' Joan wrote in December 1964. 'That is what we are all there for and I feel thankful if our talk helped you to get yourself sorted out.' Desmond's different plans and projects for Castle Leslie were all discussed with members of the lodge, who offered comfort each time another scheme failed to come to fruition. 'I am very pleased to hear your news about the unfolding plan for your work,' Grace Cooke told him in February 1968. 'White Eagle assures me that the "Brothers" are aware of all the trials and tests, but there must come the right time for right action. It will come.' He could even discuss his marital difficulties without fear of censure. 'We are so very sorry to hear of the trouble with Agi,' Joan remarked in 1968. 'It certainly is a sad tangle and I have put all your names on the Altar, with Glaslough, and know that somehow the magic will work.' Thirteen years later, she was able to reassure Desmond,

> It is by no accident, dear Aton, that you have been placed as you are in the heart of Ireland as the focal point for the Star in that beautiful country. You have ancient links with your country, and the Brothers of the Light are looking to you to be a strong, clear channel. Now, do not feel sad and despairing at this and think that you are no good. You are a very important link in the chain of light around the world.

Because there was no need to defend or justify himself, throughout his correspondence with the White Eagle Lodge Desmond's tone is modest and self-effacing with none of the bluster he could display elsewhere. 'Your kind rays have already helped a lot,' he told Joan Hodgson the following April.

> The only thing I must make clear is that I have no spiritual folies de grandeur. I have never seen myself as a great soul with a mission or any of that nonsense … Somewhere between being told I have a great mission and being told I'm a backward nit, there lies a simple normal person who I think I am about to find. This simple ordinary person wants only to practise his talents that God gave him, and be himself, and to add his little mite to the general good.

Gradually he ascended through the different stages of membership, officially joining the White Eagle Lodge in 1968, being accepted into the Outer Brotherhood in 1971 and then the Inner two years later. One of the key features of the organization has always been its belief in spiritual healing, accomplished through the thought-projection of colour rays to the psychic centres, or chakras, of an individual's body. The process, it is proposed, can be undertaken by either direct contact with the person concerned or through Absent Healing. As the organization's own literature explains, Absent Healing

> is given by groups each consisting of six healers under the leadership of one who is a member of White Eagle's Inner Brotherhood and specially trained in the projection of healing power by thought and prayer ... The soul of the patient is alerted and linked to the healing centre by the calling of the full name which sets up a powerful vibration in the invisible ether. Healing rays of light and colour prescribed by White Eagle are then poured onto that soul through the thought and prayer of the sitters in the group.

Desmond regularly asked for Absent Healing, usually for people of his acquaintance he knew to be unwell or unhappy, but sometimes for larger groups or even the entire island of Ireland. In March 1971, for example, Joan Hodgson wrote to him, 'I am sure that it will help and comfort you to know that not only in the Brotherhood on Monday, but every day at the noon service, we are holding your beloved Ireland in the blazing Christ Star, and I have no doubt that gradually the angels of peace will triumph.' Likewise the following January her mother Grace Cooke reassured Desmond, 'We are doing our very utmost to help the situation in Ireland, and I am convinced that the White Brotherhood are watching over the country and all their brothers and workers therein.' Very gradually indeed, because in January 1984 Desmond requested, 'Can you hold the whole town and district of Monaghan in the light for the next few weeks? The rough bouncers at the local disco bashed the hell out of some provos a while back. A masked gang descended on one of the bouncers' houses at Christmas (so Christian!) and shot him dead … we fear gang warfare.'

Desmond periodically went on week-long 'retreats' to Newlands, the White Eagle Lodge's headquarters in Hampshire, and always returned feeling refreshed. 'There are times when words no longer have any valid meaning,' he told Grace and Ivan Cooke in August 1972 after spending time with them, 'and it would be quite impossible to try and use mere words to describe the unforgettable week at Newlands. Perhaps I can only say that I spent it looking forward to and delighting in a non-stop series of celestial treats.' Later, however, he started to find these retreats overly sociable for his taste,

Desmond and Antonia c.1965–6. Desmond is wearing the famous dressing gown that was worn by Senator Bertie Pell when he was US Ambassador in Budapest and received Austria-Hungary's declaration of war.

describing them in October 1982 as 'getting too noisy, and more like a nice country house party than a time of deep religious experience. That endless small talk and silly giggly conversations ...' But by that time Desmond had found an alternative to visiting Newlands: with the approval of the White Eagle leadership, he had established his own group based at Castle Leslie, the first in Ireland. Here, in a room set aside for the purpose in one of the wings, he could hold his own prayer services (disturbed only by noise from his young daughters Sammy and Camilla who were playing directly below), explain the nature of the White Eagle Lodge to anyone interested, and engage in Direct Healing. As far back as June 1968, he and Helen had organized a week-long retreat for a disparate assortment of friends on Lusty Beg, an island on Lough Erne in County Fermanagh. 'When the mood seemed right,' he informed Joan Hodgson, 'I read White Eagle's passages on Venus in Wisdom ... and I played the White Eagle record – the first time his voice has been heard in Ireland. I don't know if there is a mantra contained within it but it always has the most extraordinary effect – of soothing people down and giving them a blissful night's sleep.' It also had other, more unexpected, consequences since a number of children – including Camilla Leslie – were conceived during that week on the appropriately named Lusty Beg.

Desmond saw the future of his family home connected in some way with the White Eagle Lodge, perhaps because its leaders provided him with such unwavering support. Staying at Newlands in June 1964, he received the following message from White Eagle, via a session with Grace Cooke:

> The beautiful home in the country has a high destiny. It may have to pass through a process of cleansing. There may be initial vicissitudes, but we assure you that if you hold *your ideal* of a beautifully cared for and preserved estate, it will eventually become as the Masters' Estate. You, dear brother, will be the

channel to commence a work for the blessing of humanity, but those who follow after you, your own children and descendants, will carry forward into the future this work ... You must preserve and hold the estate in *your own power* until the time is ripe for the Brethren ... The invisible Brethren will help you. Be guided by your own inner light, by the Truth within you when you feel it is right, take action but not unless.

Later that year he received another message from White Eagle, this time posted to Castle Leslie by Joan Hodgson: 'I know that Glaslough can grow into a beautiful centre of light and healing, but it will only do so with hard work and dedication ...'

Desmond's engagement with the White Eagle Lodge reflected his broader interests in spirituality and religious faith, subjects that continued to fascinate him long after he had found a form of belief tailored to his specific requirements. But he could not return to the Roman Catholicism of his youth, not even for the sake of his old mentor, Fr Oswald Vanheems. As he informed the latter in October 1963, 'I fully understand your views and believe me I respect them. I respect and admire your way of life, your hard work, your sacrifice, and I know that in this one short lifetime you will climb high up the ladder that leads to perfection.' However, despite his respect Desmond had to inform Fr Oswald:

I only know that the White Eagle group who are some of the finest and most integrated human beings I have ever been privileged to meet saved my life and my marriage. Without their gentle guidance and spiritual healing at a time when Agnes and I had to 'walk the valley of death' and know total darkness, these kindly beings unobtrusively helped us when we were on the brink of hell.

Eventually, of course, not even the support of the White Eagle Lodge was enough to save Desmond's first marriage, but he remained loyal to the group, not least because as the Troubles in Northern Ireland grew steadily worse, the established Christian denominations all came to look so unattractive. 'As you know,' he told his son Sean in September 1975,

> I do not believe any religion on this absurd planet is anywhere near the real truth nor is any being on this earth capable of perceiving it at our low stage of development. Even my beloved White Eagle Lodge whose wisdom still staggers me would be the first to admit their knowledge was anything more than an inkling, and that there is not and never can be any 'final revelation'. We just go on growing and growing, ever (with lapses) coming closer to God, while He manifests to us on our own level in guises we can understand and recognise in all nature, all life and – most perfectly – through Jesus.

Jesus was the subject of a book Desmond published in 1975, his first serious work since *The Amazing Mr Lutterworth* seventeen years earlier. Like *Flying Saucers Have Landed*, *The Jesus File* involved an enormous amount of research because Desmond chose to tell the story of Christ's death and resurrection as though it were a dossier compiled by diverse members of the Roman Imperial civil service. As late as May 1974 he was still struggling with the book, telling Ivan Cooke it needed a lot of rewriting. 'There's so much to be said and so many alternative ways of saying it. The work must be perfect, and I'm dissatisfied with so much of it. It has to be RIGHT before release to the thirsty ones!'

Released the following year, *The Jesus File* met with a decidedly mixed response from critics. In the Irish current affairs magazine *Hibernia*, fellow writer Wolf Mankowitz was enthusiastic, describing Desmond as 'without doubt an Irish original in the grand tradition of inspired eccentricity and institution-mocking which goes back, I suppose, to Dean Swift and then beyond Swift to those Celtic court poets whose sharp ironic observations could bring blood to the cheek'. But then again, Mankowitz was a friend of Desmond and at the time was living in one of Castle Leslie's gate lodges, so his opinion could hardly be considered untainted. More objectively, writing in *The Church Times* Rosamond Essex called the book 'Scholarly; fascinating; impelling. It is not usual to be able to use all three adjectives about a religious book. But it can be said, in my estimation, about this one … Here is one of the most intensely interesting books I have read for some time.' Likewise the *Cork Examiner*'s unnamed reviewer considered *The Jesus File* 'a deeply moving novel of unusual conviction and strength'.

On the other hand, writing in *The Irish Times*, Jeananne Crowley thought, 'This book is a quasi-religious, queasy commercial endeavour set in an idiom I have come to know and dread, but one in which most men seem to find a special fascination. The world of secrets, official and otherwise, special investigators, police interrogation, trial transcripts and army orders.' Similarly in *The Guardian* Robert Nye judged the book, 'more than eccentric and less than good'.

The fundamental problem with *The Jesus File* lies not in its form but its subject matter. The fact was that the time when publications of this sort received a broad readership had passed: Desmond's interest in and engagement with religion did not reflect the general mood of an age growing steadily more secular in outlook. Investigations into the final days of Christ on this earth were therefore likely to win the notice only of committed Christians, which is why the religious media broadly welcomed the book and the general press did not. Still, despite her disparaging review, Jeananne Crowley and Desmond subsequently became friends, thereby indicating he was not a man to take offence at criticism.

Besides, though intermittently subject to depression, Desmond continued to possess a strong and restorative sense of humour, something very necessary for a man in his position during the 1970s and 1980s. Often this humour found expression in his correspondence, such as the letter sent to members of the White Eagle Lodge, which was headed: 'Ireland's Swinging Schloss. Ghosts by the Night or by the Hour. Poltergeists extra, less 15% cash discount. Natural Air-conditioning in every Turret. Running Water throughout All Ceilings. No children, no dogs, no banshees, no hawkers, no bottles. Proprietors: La Belle Helene, and Prof. Dr Desmond Leslie.' In October 1980, he wrote to a bank manager who had demanded that Desmond should repay a loan that 'It is only out of my boundless charity that I keep my overdraft going. A terrible vision came upon me of starving bankers cadging for crusts in the dustbins of Clubland, for *everyone* had repaid his borrowings, leaving the poor souls with no income. Verily, had Nemesis struck.'

Desmond's sense of humour also found an outlet in a slim book he co-authored in 1972 with his friend, the astronomer Patrick Moore. In style and spirit *How Britain Won the Space Race* reads like a published episode of *Monty Python's Flying Circus*, simultaneously mocking and celebrating the traditional British character. With illustrations derived from mid-nineteenth-century editions of the *Illustrated London News*, it purports to show how a small band of plucky Englishmen led by the fictional Sir Humphrey ffryde-Fischer managed to land a craft on the moon just one day before the American Apollo 11 actually did so on 21 July 1969 and Neil Armstrong became the first man to walk on its surface. According to *How Britain Won the Space Race*, Sir Humphrey and his team touched down in their British Orbital Space Station on 20 July and immediately installed four 'Losby Uprichard Tea Boilers' as well as a billiard table and practice cricket net. Running to just fifty pages, it's a joke extended almost to breaking point but remains entertaining in a charmingly adolescent way, as though Desmond and Patrick Moore were two public schoolboys who found it funny to write of the fictional British space explorers, 'Their means were limited. So, for that matter, were their brains,' and thought it hilarious to invent names like Gottfried von Doppelganger and Herr Doktor Silenus

Schrimpwisl who, from his laboratory 'threw himself whole-heartedly into his work. On one occasion he also threw himself into the sea, together with the shattered parts of his pioneer rocket, code name NUTS (Nuclear Unguided Test Ship).'

Desmond's abiding humour and amusing conversation also helped to win him a wide circle of friends throughout his time at Castle Leslie. Many of the people with whom he socialized were living in similar circumstances such as Harry and Camilla, Earl and Countess Erne, whose home was on the other side of the border at Crom Castle, County Fermanagh. Desmond and Helen spent the New Year of 1973 with the Ernes and afterwards he wrote to his brother Jack, 'People have started giving parties and going out again, with a sort of "to hell with them all" feeling, rather like after the Blitz in England.'

Four years later, the couple – together with their daughters Sammy and Camilla – went to County Galway for Christmas when they stayed at Lough Cutra Castle; originally designed in the early 19th century by John Nash for the first Viscount Gort, the house had recently been bought and restored by Tim Gwyn-Jones. On the eve of festivities, Desmond subsequently informed Grace Cooke,

> all the Christmas tree lights went wrong and so I was asked to fix it (which I eventually did) by which time it was 5 to 12 and champagne was flowing in all directions … Lunchtime December 29, clouds of black smoke from the clock tower and I jokily remarked the good ship was getting up steam; the boiler went and fortunately in a separate tower so the only real hazard was no hot water nor heating. So we moved on to my sister in her mediaeval tower at Oranmore in Galway – beautifully centrally heated but the wee man who delivered oil was drunk and we had to ferry it in 5-gallon cans from her stables … When you get on a plane at Heathrow and fly to Ireland you spend 55 minutes in the air but you put your watches back 100 years. It is part of the charm – also the tragedy of Ireland.

But if Desmond and Helen were occasionally guests in someone else's home, much more often they found themselves playing
the part of hosts at Castle Leslie, which witnessed a constant stream
of visitors, some more famous than others. Among the best-known
was Mick Jagger, who called by in August 1968 with then-girlfriend
Marianne Faithfull to ask about the possibility of renting Castle Leslie for a couple of months. Though the money would have been
attractive, Desmond turned down the opportunity, explaining the
house was his family home. 'My own feeling is that your difficult
decision *re* the Rolling Stone gentleman and his girlfriend was the
right one,' Ivan Cooke advised. 'You don't know what kind of chaos
you might have returned to after the event …'

But Mick Jagger stayed long enough to run into a group of
girls who had come to Castle Leslie on a day's outing from their
approved school across the border. Chaperoned by nuns, the party
was reasonably well-behaved until some of the girls spotted the singer

Mick Jagger with schoolgirls at Castle Leslie in 1968.

swimming nude in the lake. When eventually allowed to emerge from the water, he took refuge at the top of the church tower but finally descended to sign autographs; invariably these were in ink on the girls' arms and shoulders. Weeks later, Desmond received a distressed call from the convent's Mother Superior saying, 'What am I to do? The girls refuse to wash!'

For a while in the early 1970s, he and Helen also hosted a colony of what he called 'neo-hippies' in the old agent's house, the building just inside the main entrance gates that had briefly served some years earlier as Annabel's on the Bog. This group used to attend his White Eagle Lodge services, despite Desmond's concern that 'it gave them almost too high a shot of energy, resulting in them having a very romantic two days while we were away in Dublin; they said "the love vibes were terrific" '. All went well until March 1971 when a friend of one of the neo-hippies was stopped by police in Belfast and found to be carrying a large quantity of LSD. Under interrogation he gave Castle Leslie as his intended destination. 'The situation now,' Desmond told Joan Hodgson, 'is that the original three couples and their children may stay on probation, but if there is any recurrence I shall reluctantly have to throw them out to avoid scandal and trouble.' A week later, he decided it would be best if the group left. 'I was sorry to see them go,' he confessed to Joan's sister Ylana Hayward. 'They are gentle souls but too much pot and acid seems to have made them spiritually "limp", is the best word to describe it … They gave us a lovely farewell supper and left at dawn (with a number of our blankets, sheets, etc – which I regard as my farewell present).' Desmond, it seems, was at last beginning to be sensible.

TWELVE

'SIXTIETH BIRTHDAY TODAY,' Desmond wrote to Joan Hodgson on 29 June 1981, 'and part of me still feels and thinks like a teenager. Sixty glorious misspent years!' He went on to describe the day itself, beginning in the morning when, as he ironically phrased it,

> the loyal peasantry in a spontaneous outburst arrived and mowed the overgrown squierarchal lawns. Polite and respectful cards were received from No. 1 Wife, Nos. 1 & 2 Sons, rude ones from Daughters Nos. 4 & 5, a bottle of whiskey from the publican (the rich man) at my gate. About noon, the Squire was carried out in his ivory and gilt sedan chair to a dais in the Gt. Forecourt where he graciously acknowledged the humble salutations of the devoted peasantry, and the simple humble gifts of the bour-geoisie. About 2.30 he opened a foundation stone and declared a local hospital well and truly laid. In the evening, the horses were lined up for approval and the Squierarchal Household moved in

order of precedence to the Riding Club where the dutiful members and minions had prepared a splendid repast laced with about 6 bottles of Pol Roget, after which selected and honoured guests were invited back to the Castle where for once a fire had been lighted in honour of the occasion where they remained in a state of rapture until the momentous evening drew to a close.

Though cheerful enough on his actual birthday, for much of the time Desmond was less inclined to rhapsodize about the joys of growing older. At sixty, his gusto for life was not what it had once been. Nor could he drive himself so hard. In August 1980 he'd told Joan there remained 'So much I want to do; ought to do; must do, but cannot do because the physical energy just isn't there.' Approaching old age, 'I find I hang onto the mane of my horse at big jumps: a sure sign of creeping decrepitude.' Skiing in the Alps with his three daughters six months beforehand, he wrote to Jack that he had found Camilla – then not yet eleven – acting as

> my guide on the long runs and waiting patiently for me at the end of each horrendous descent. When she calmly announced at lunch she'd just done the Olympic downhill speed run, I had no alternative but to ask her to escort me down it that afternoon if I was to save face. I managed to reach the bottom reasonably intact after three-quarters of an hour. The record is one and three-quarter minutes!

Desmond was also more prone to grow cranky and irritable than had previously been the case, informing Joan Hodgson in December 1981 that he had come to dislike loud noise and trivial chatter. 'Living here in the beautiful silence of nature affects one. I've said just about all I have to say. I've heard just about everything our dear neighbours have to say … The things I'd like to talk about, they don't wish to hear. The things they want to prattle on about bore me.' What increasingly interested him were his horses and the equestrian centre he had established on the estate. From childhood onwards Desmond had been a keen horseman but only in these years did he finally put his enthusiasm to practical use. In the 1970s, he had once more taken up hunting, albeit his own interpretation of the sport. As he explained to Joan after a meet at Castle Leslie in April 1970, his hunts were

> a mixture of a mini-Badminton, sardines and catch as can. I was the 'fox' wearing a white coat and given three minutes start on my horse. The object was to throw the pack off the scent and having done so to tootle away on the horn to lure them back again. When one of them caught me he would join my pack until the whole field had reunited. The last to catch us became the next 'fox'. It was a terrifically fast run, cross country, over hedges, ditches, fences, through woods; really much more exciting than working with hounds who always get lost and go the wrong way and take days to catch afterwards. Everyone said it was the greatest sport and I'm hoping it will catch on. It has always seemed to me possible to enjoy the thrill of a fast chase without having to hunt some poor animal.

The following October, writing to the founding editor of *Psychic News*, Maurice Barbanell, he described a similar meet on the estate:

> Not only are no poor animals involved (except the horses who thoroughly enjoy themselves and snort with excitement) but you get a far better route and run, for the 'quarry' can select all the best gallops on the most tricky and exacting chases ... We could not think what to call this new bloodless sport. After the last meet, the old MFH got it: 'The Hunting of the Snark'.

More such hunts were held at Castle Leslie over the next couple of years until Desmond and Helen decided to develop the estate into an equestrian centre, which opened in the mid-1970s. It was the latest, and by far the most successful, of the many money-making ventures in which he had been involved since moving back to Ireland in 1963. The Castle Leslie Equestrian Centre, or CLEC, was based just inside the main gates in the old Agent's House, now renamed the Hunting Lodge and with its interior converted to accommodate guests. What, a decade earlier, had been Annabel's on the Bog now became a club bar called Fence Fifty, which, as Desmond noted in a publicity brochure, 'is one fence that has never known a refusal'. Around the estate he planned and created what was claimed to be the largest cross-country course in Europe: in all twenty-five miles with two hundred varied fences. In fact, Desmond's design featured not just one course, but a complex sequence of them that could be explored either individually or in a variety of combinations, with the option of 'everything from leisurely hacking to fast competitive stuff over a tremendous variety of fences'.

A feature in *The Northern Standard* of 23 December 1976 highlighted a course called The Big Ride: 'A ten-mile group ride through woods, fields and streams, over every type of obstacle, natural and prepared, designed to suit the skill or lack of it of any rider, with always a discreet gate for non-jumpers.' There was also a dauntingly big jump called The Kraut Basher, for German clients who were a little too confident of their own abilities. Writing about his new venture, Desmond observed how one of its distinctive features of the centre was that 'riding is treated as FUN. Hunts, clubs and groups are coming in increasing numbers. Hunts, bored with barbed wire, cross farmers and scentless days, come here knowing they'll get a run, and a damned good one – as fast and as long as they or their mounts can take.'

Despite its proximity to the border with Northern Ireland CLEC began to attract a steady clientele, especially among groups of Northern Europeans who soon accounted for more than 60 per cent of its annual turnover. Guests were offered the opportunity to enjoy at least four hours' riding every day, with the additional option of pike fishing on the Castle Leslie lake. Once a week, Desmond and Helen would host a drinks party in the main house, followed by a barbeque if weather permitted. And for non-riders, as another of the centre's brochures promised, 'there are beautiful walks round the lakes, bird

Castle Leslie Equestrian Centre programme.

sanctuaries, wild deer strongholds, and miles of superb scenery to be explored and enjoyed'. In 1979 the enterprise won a tourism award from the United Dominions Trust 'For the Best Individual Effort'. It also garnered plenty of positive press attention, with Kevin Myers in the January/February 1979 edition of *Ireland of the Welcomes* describing CLEC as 'the St Moritz of equestrianism'. In *Horse and Hound* later that same year, Jane McIlvaine McClary waxed lyrical about the 'gorgeous galloping and jumping over peerless scenery ... satiny fields that practically shouted to be ridden over'.

Given that the Castle Leslie Equestrian Centre was reasonably successful and showed every prospect of becoming even more so over time, it is surprising to discover that by 1982 Desmond had entered discussions to sell the business. Finally, after almost twenty years of setbacks, he could begin to look forward to a better and more prosperous future were he to persevere with the enterprise. And yet, just as he had found a winning formula, he chose to let go of the equestrian centre he'd developed. The explanation for his bizarre behaviour seems to lie in something already mentioned: Desmond's age and growing sense of fatigue. For almost twenty years, in addition to all the turmoils of his personal life, he had battled with a variety of banks and solicitors and accountants and civil servants in order to retain possession of Castle Leslie. The effort had worn him out. While the equestrian centre could have been further expanded and developed, and very possibly built into a profitable concern, he no longer had the stamina for such an enterprise. Better to let someone younger and fitter take on the challenge and allow him to rest. Although his daughter Sammy had just qualified as a riding instructor, he felt that at eighteen she was still too young to take on the mantle.

Initially there was talk of Robert Gloag, who had been managing the centre for some time, assuming a bigger role. Then Desmond opened negotiations with Equitour, a Swiss company that had sent many riding groups to Castle Leslie, for the sale not just of the business but also the Hunting Lodge, its outbuildings and stables. But when this proposal failed to come to fruition, he arranged to sell the whole business instead to Geraldine Bellew, who had previously run the stables for Desmond. The transaction concluded, the Bellews reopened as the Greystones Equestrian Centre and Desmond ought to have been able to retire to the house and enjoy the rest he deserved. But, as on so many previous occasions, he soon found himself in conflict, this time with the centre's new owners and also his nephew Tarka King, in both cases due to disputes over access rights across the estate.

It would take many years, and yet more expensive litigation, before the arguments were satisfactorily resolved. In the meantime,

Desmond remained as much as ever in need of ready money; after many years of neglect, the fabric of Castle Leslie itself was starting to deteriorate. His daughter Sammy later remembered a childhood in which sections of the house had to be closed off as they fell into disrepair, beginning with the basement, followed by the wings. The old billiard room was used to store hay for the horses and the library 'was full of junk'. On the upper floors, there was always the risk of leaks whenever it rained. One of Sammy Leslie's earliest memories was 'the sight of all the buckets – to catch the drips … the leaks dictated where we slept'. In November 1976 Desmond informed Jack, 'The damn leak has started in the Schoolroom again and I had to rip up a funnel and hosepipe leading out through the window to get rid of the inrush. Such a pest …' With almost no staff to help them and with an estate and equestrian centre to manage, Desmond and Helen had little time left to care for the big old house and by New Year 1982 he could tell Joan Hodgson the family had spent

> a jolly traditional Christmas here with freezes, burst pipes, floods and all the merrie yuletide accessories. But at last I have discovered the secrets of this vast antediluvian water system and know which vast valve, cock or knob to turn depending whether I want to isolate the footman's loo in the N. Wing or the Under Housekeeper's sewing room in the basement or the H&C for both which, of course, run their separate ways.

This was Desmond in relatively upbeat mood, but living with constant cold and discomfort, and without any prospect of imminent relief, grew to be a joyless experience and he sometimes subsided into despondency. The family retreated to one small section of the house from where they observed the rest slipping further into decay. Wood-burning stoves were installed in their own quarters; these were lit 'if anyone can be persuaded to cut and hump wet branches that have recently fallen in the garden', wrote Desmond in a memorandum detailing Castle Leslie's problems, 'the rest of the house is an energy-saving, environmentally-friendly deep freeze, which is why no one with any pulmonary troubles can survive there in winter'. Extensive dry rot was discovered in the main reception areas while

> the drainage from the middle roof falls down the disused lift shaft and floods the basement unless the leaves and dead frogs etc are continually removed from a rather unpleasant gunk hole. The outer roofs are precipitously pitched at 65 degrees, making gutters, spouting and hoppers extremely difficult to clean and to keep unblocked. It only requires one overflow to set up another patch of dry rot.

Since the disposal of the Bassano oil in 1971 additional works of art had been sold at auction and in order to preserve the structure from further dilapidation this continued to be necessary. In 1988 Desmond was obliged to sell a marble bust of Christ that had been in the house since brought there by the first Sir John Leslie more than a century earlier. Originally carved around 1595 by the Florentine sculptor Giovanni Caccini for the church of Santa Maria Novella, funds from its sale temporarily relieved Desmond of his financial burdens; the bust is now in the collection of Amsterdam's Rijksmuseum.

With each sale, whether of land or timber or outbuildings or house contents, Desmond further diminished the value of his core asset but he was caught in a bind and unable to do anything else. What mattered was that the house itself, together with as much surrounding land as possible, should be preserved for the next generation. This became ever more important as Desmond grew older and began to give consideration to what might happen to Castle Leslie after his death. He also started to worry about the circumstances of his two youngest children, Sammy and Camilla. They had been born in 1966 and 1969 respectively, when he and Helen were unmarried. The year after Camilla's birth, Desmond obtained a divorce from Agnes in Mexico and married Helen in England, but neither of these actions had any validity in Ireland where according

Desmond in the mid-1980s.

to the law Agnes remained his wife and Sammy and Camilla were deemed illegitimate. This meant they had no succession rights.

As the girls entered their teens and he approached his sixtieth birthday, Desmond grew anxious about their future. His initial concern was over the trust established by Anne Bourke Cockran in 1945, and what should happen to his share of this resource when he died. As he wrote to Knox Ide, a New York cousin – and Anne Bourke Cockran's executor – in September 1980, his aunt's will 'states very simply that upon my death the principal shall be divided equally between "my children". It does not qualify the words which I seem to remember were "and upon his death to his children in equal parts". It does not say his legitimate children, nor the children of his marriage or anything else, just "his children" '. Desmond wanted to know whether Sammy and Camilla would be included under the terms of Anne Bourke Cockran's will or whether he needed to make separate provision for them. The following month, a partner in his cousin's law firm replied that according to his interpretation of the will, the two girls 'are entitled to share in the principal of the trust under Anne Cockran's will upon your death only if they would be considered legitimate children of yours under Irish law as it was in force in 1945' (the year in which Anne Cockran had died). If this were not the case, he recommended, 'there may be some action you could take', but the question 'can best be answered by Irish counsel'.

There followed many years of legal analysis, discussion and wrangling over the status of Sammy and Camilla Leslie. Eventually it was concluded that if the girls were to be officially recognized in Ireland as the children of Desmond and Helen they would have to be adopted. However, a further problem then arose because the Irish State did not recognize the 1970 marriage and Desmond and Helen were therefore not eligible to adopt as a legally married couple. But as an unmarried couple they were equally ineligible. 'The alternative,' advised Desmond's solicitor in September 1984, 'would be for you alone to adopt the children. This has one significant disadvantage. It would mean that Helen must surrender all her parental rights to you, and while the children would then, for example, have rights under the Succession Act to your Estate, they would lose their rights under the Succession Act to a share in Helen's Estate.' Understandably Helen was extremely unhappy with this proposal and the matter dragged on.

In January 1987 Desmond's solicitor suggested he obtain another divorce from Agnes and then remarry Helen, this time in France, 'which would be recognised by the Irish State' since the marriage laws had grown somewhat more relaxed by this date. A fresh divorce would also serve another purpose, since as the solicitor noted, on Desmond's death, 'In my opinion your Mexican divorce would not be so recognised, and accordingly Agnes would be entitled to claim a Legal Right Share to one third of your Free Estate.' A re-divorce and remarriage did not happen and in the end, so as to secure their inheritance rights and despite Helen's justifiable misgivings, Desmond did adopt his own two children. By the time this finally happened, Sammy was legally classified as an adult.

THIRTEEN

THE RIDICULOUS COMPLICATIONS involved in his effort to secure inheritance rights for Sammy and Camilla undoubtedly coloured Desmond's attitude towards Ireland in his last years. Mocking the absurdities of life in the country now became a feature of his writing during this period. At the time of a political scandal in 1983 when former Minister for Justice Seán Doherty was implicated in tapping the telephones of two journalists, Desmond wrote a letter to newspapers saying he failed to understand what all the fuss was about, given that most Irish exchanges continued the tradition of being manually operated. 'Until recently when we went automatic,' he elaborated,

> we had a bugging service second to none. In a small rural community this has many advantages. For example (1) it ensures instant dissemination of the latest village gossip and (2) does

away with the necessity of having to repeat it (3) provides an up-to-date information service on the social and geographic movements of local citizenry. Suppose I phone the MacAs to ask them to dinner on Tuesday and receive no reply, the friendly and much-loved voice informs me that it's no use ringing them till *Dallas* is over, or that I can save my money and not make the call, for they are going to the MacBs next Tuesday …

Desmond became a keen letter-writer, especially to *The Irish Times* where his sardonic missives were often printed. In September 1974, after yet another debate in Ireland over Radio Telefís Éireann playing the Angelus on air, he proposed that not only should the national broadcasting service abandon this twice-daily Catholic devotional exercise but that it ought to be closed down, 'For the very use of television and radio is artificial and every bit as much against the Natural Law as contraception. Surely, if God had intended a buffoon in Donnybrook to be simultaneously seen and heard in Donegal and Dublin, He would have ordered matters accordingly?' Almost two years later, he noted that

> The Minister for Lands recently expressed his disquiet concerning the irresponsible behaviour by a minority of visitors coming to Ireland for shooting. I think he is misinformed. I don't know about ordinary visitor shoots, but I do know that at all the foreign industrialist and banker shoots I've attended, the blighters have behaved perfectly; running straight down the line of guns, not too high, not too low, presenting perfect targets for even the worst shot. Of course, anyone who couldn't hit a German banker, couldn't hit anything …

Given his circumstances, official interference in rural life particularly tended to infuriate Desmond, as when in December 1986 he wrote to *The Irish Times* about the current Minister for Agriculture's concern over the possibility that badgers were responsible for the spread of tuberculosis. Not so, argued Desmond. In fact, 'The only really dangerous species today, without which the world would be infinitely more wholesome, is "Politicianus Gombeenius" which should most certainly be wiped out.' And in a similar vein, in October 1991 he informed readers of the paper's letters page that he was

a keen supporter of the following blood sports. Mass shoots of all truly repellent life forms, such as international arms dealers and bankers. The coursing of politicians by ravenous wolves. Barbecues of badger-baiters (Spectators would not be required actually to eat the remains; these would be offered to the less discerning carnivores in the zoo). Manhunts of speculators, developers, bureaucrats and similar subspecies of Homo Insipiens. The total extinction of imbeciles who cannot go for a nice country walk without wanting to kill something … In conclusion, wild birds and wild life are more attractive than most humans. Anyone in doubt should look in the mirror.

But one of Desmond's particular concerns was what he perceived to be the increasingly retrogressive ideology of the Roman Catholic Church in Ireland. In November 1989, for example, he wrote to *The Irish Times* questioning the church's objection to the ordination of women priests and proposing that in the Old Testament's *Book* of Genesis God was a woman.

God-the-Mother was widely accepted in the Middle East, viz: 'The Great Mother, She who by Her power brought Order out of Chaos' (early Sumerian fragment), And for many centuries the Holy Spirit was feminine (Mother), until the good fathers in their wisdom changed Sophia into a little white bird (last seen at the river Jordan and in Act III *Parsifal*).

This letter reveals Desmond's wide reading on and knowledge of many cultures and faiths that had informed his earlier books, most especially *Flying Saucers Have Landed*. Now he decided to put this ~~~~ted data to use in a new work, called *What a Way to Run ~~~~* script it is an enormous, sprawling text that fills three volumes, a philosophical treatise displaying Desmond's considerable erudition but also his need for a good editor who could have curtailed the author's speculations and perambulations. Running from an analysis of Sanskrit texts to a discourse on the character of papal infallibility, *What a Way to Run a Universe* reflects his understanding of world religions both extant and extinct, his interest in spiritualism and psychic mediums, his belief in reincarnation, even his experience with recorded music. Although full of fascinating material, ultimately what it lacks is a clear sense of coherence or purpose. To some extent it is an apologia for the White Eagle Lodge: one chapter is devoted to discussing the organization's Five Great Laws and towards the end of the first volume Desmond wrote that through the work of the White Eagle Lodge, 'the Great Consolation is slowly but surely coming back into the world … Knowledge of our true immortality will take away so much that is frantic and fearful in our lives.'

But though the White Eagle Lodge is discussed and praised, no more than any other faith does it provide a central doctrine for *What a Way to Run a Universe*. The book reflects Desmond's own divergent concerns, prominent among them his disaffection with the Roman Catholic faith in which he had been raised, and with most organized religions as well as with the concept of a single God who 'finds contraceptives sinful, and cervical rings positively murderous, but raises no objection to one lot of his children marching off to murder another lot of his children provided they wear the correct fancy dress for the purpose'. Above all, *What a Way to Run a Universe* is an attempt to discover the purpose of humanity's existence, with life on earth being

> either all a big accident, caring not a hoot, with Man the most
> freakish accident of all. Or it is run by an insane or irresponsi-
> ble potentate; and because of the inescapable nastiness of this
> surmise, many kindly and devout people have been led to reject

the idea of any sort of God at the helm, turning sadly, often with despair in their heart, to the dogma of materialism. It could well be summed up in the couplet: If God is God he is not good / If God is good he is not God.

Desmond's preoccupations were unlikely to engage anyone else to quite the same degree. He took enormous trouble over this latest book, writing to Grace Cooke in January 1976 that the work

> proceeds sloggingly and slowly. How fantastically difficult it is to write simple truth simply … One knows what one wants to say, but to say it so it will be understood by the unknowing is so very hard … there must be about 200,000 words waiting to be organised and reorganised and pruned and repolished. Rather like building a temple and the contractor delivers ALL the materials in a huge higgledy-piggledy heap, and you have to sort them out and fit them together.

Despite the vast amount of effort Desmond put into its preparation, with many sections rewritten over and over again, *What a Way to Run a Universe* was unpublished and is likely to remain so.

Sadly the same is true of another of his literary enterprises from this period. In 1979 English author and illustrator Kit Williams created a book called *Masquerade*, based around a treasure hunt for a jewelled golden hare he had buried in the countryside. Hundreds of thousands of copies were sold and a worldwide search began for the prize, which was eventually discovered only three years later (by fraudulent means, it subsequently transpired).

The success of *Masquerade* inspired an entire genre of books known as armchair treasure hunts, one of which was written by Desmond from an idea that had come from his friend, antique dealer Alan Chawner. *Find the Crock of Gold* was compiled in 1983 and described in a prospectus as 'a wonderful children's story and treasure hunt'. The tale concerned two Irish elves called Puck and Pog charged with guarding the crock of gold lying at the end of the rainbow. One day they lose control of the rainbow, which, along with its gold, vanishes and has to be tracked down. Puck and Pog – together with the reader – embark on this quest, meeting many adventures along the way. As for the treasure hunt, it came with an initial prize of £2000 in gold which would be increased by 2.5 per cent of the retail price for every book sold, 'thus making the potential prize absolutely enormous'. Like *Masquerade*, the book was gloriously illustrated – by a young Dublin-born artist called Gerard Glynn whose work Desmond considered to be 'a cross between Rackham and Bosch, and far more imaginative than Kit Williams'. However, although both text and pictures were completed and a dummy copy prepared, this was another project destined not to come to fruition.

So much effort, so little reward. By the late 1980s, Desmond's strength started to fail. Although still only in his mid-sixties, he was exhausted after so many years of struggle. Helen had inherited a property in the South of France high above Nice from her mother, and she and Desmond began spending more and more of their time there: the climate was kinder, the demands on both of them less strenuous. Their daughter Sammy remembers an especially harsh Irish winter when Desmond spent months dressed in a grey ski suit to keep himself warm.

In 1987, he and Helen officially moved to France, although like his father before him, Desmond continued to make an annual pilgrimage to Castle Leslie. 'He really wanted to live in Ireland but couldn't,' says Sammy. 'He loved France, but he'd no craic there. He missed Ireland terribly.' Ill health obliged Desmond to relinquish his control of Castle Leslie; had he died suddenly while still in possession of the property, taxes would have forced its sale by his heirs. The plan was that the house and estate would be invested in a trust in the names of his five children by Agnes and Helen. But there were complications and suspicions and uncertainties, and in 1991 the notion

Mark, Antonia and Sean outside Castle Leslie, at Luke Leslie's christening, 1987.

of a trust was abandoned. By then Sammy, who had trained as a riding instructor and been running the Castle Leslie stables before backpacking around the world and studying hotel management in Switzerland, had expressed an interest in taking over responsibility for the estate's future. In 1991, Desmond handed over the estate to his five children by Agnes and Helen. In March of the following year he wrote, 'Darling Sammy, I am so happy that you love Glaslough enough to try and work it, otherwise there would not be much point in keeping it. I will do everything I can to help you – you know that … If there were no inheritance taxes, I would have kept it in my name until I died. And then, at my age, have leased it to you.'

In fact, in 1995 Sammy did negotiate a lease with her four siblings that allowed her to take over the management of the estate. Circumstances in the increasingly prosperous Ireland of the mid-1990s were very different from those three decades earlier and many of the projects planned and attempted by Desmond could finally be put into successful operation. The struggles he went through now seem impossibly remote, the battles he fought to hang on to Castle Leslie inconceivable. As the Troubles in Northern Ireland drew to a close and peace descended along the border shared with the Republic, Monaghan was no longer a place to be avoided. National and international funding became available for schemes designed to encourage development and employment in the region, and Sammy Leslie was in a position to take advantage of this assistance. Today Desmond's dreams for the estate have been fully realized. In line with his belief that 'we are not owners but just guardians of this very special place', Sammy subsequently set up a family trust to ensure the long-term future of the estate as home to the Leslies.

In the South of France, Desmond lived a quieter, less frenetic existence than had hitherto been the case. Much of his time was devoted to writing yet another book, a rambling *roman-fleuve* called *Pandora*. The work, he informed fellow writer Stan Gebler Davies, was 'extremely erotic, mischievous and romantic. It's a sexy book, but very loving. Sex without love is boring, like champagne without fizz. There isn't a dirty word in it except when addressing bureaucracy and those office boys in princes' seats who now misrule the world.' Originally Desmond planned to write the story of an elemental being – daughter of the pagan god Pan – who, rather like Hans Christian Anderson's Little Mermaid, wishes to become a human but can only do this by marrying a man. Before long, however, the novel went off on a variety of tangents as Desmond drew on his own experiences to write about John, Pandora's future husband, and his time at boarding school and after. John is involved with a woman psychic called Jenny, fifteen years his senior who, at the end of the first section of the book, leaves him to move to the United States where she becomes governess to the children of a wealthy east-coast family.

Meanwhile John marries for the first time, his wife being a former top model, 'a spoiled brat, with a father who plays polo with Prince Philip until he goes "inside" for insider trading', and John distracts himself with an affair with another model called Debbie Dobson who is taken to court on charges of running a brothel from her flat in London. And so it goes on, with Jenny losing her job as governess and then travelling with an architect lover to Arizona where, while sleeping out under the stars, she 'gets bitten rather painfully by some insect in a rather awkward place' before she goes to Los Angeles and is ordered to leave a hotel for exposing her breasts in public. There is much more of the same, with Desmond so interested in following the adventures he devised for Jenny and John that he rather forgets about his eponymous heroine, although she is reintroduced later in the tale. Rather in the style of the late English author Simon Raven's own *romans-fleuves*, *Pandora* is an entertaining romp filled with exaggerated characters in implausible situations. And like so much of Desmond's later work it would benefit from radical pruning but has a verve and wit surprising in a man of his age.

Particularly surprising because during his final years Desmond was in very poor health. In 1985 his sister Anita had died, as did Agnes after a long illness in February 1999. An asthmatic child, years and years of heavy smoking meant Desmond now suffered from the chronic emphysema that finally killed him. 'As kids,' Sammy recalled, 'we'd sit on his bed and listen to him wheezing. His chest sounded like bubbling hot mud.' In the millennium year 2000, aware her natural father was growing ever more frail and anxious to see him one more time while she still could, Wendyl Jay, daughter of Jennifer Phipps, booked to fly to Europe the following spring with the intention of spending a week in Ireland before she went on to the South of France. By the time she reached her second destination in mid-February 2001 Desmond was failing fast. White Eagle had told him that he would die with all six of his children around

Last photo taken of Desmond (with Sammy, left, and Camilla), 2000.

him. His two youngest daughters Camilla and Sammy were already with him, the latter having brought with her a clutch of snowdrops from Castle Leslie. Soon the rest of the immediate family, his brother Jack and children Sean, Mark and Antonia also arrived; it was the very first time they had all been in the same place together.

By now he had been moved to a public hospital in Antibes where each member of the family was granted a private audience; as Mark explained, now was the 'chance for all the things one wants to say and often regrets not saying afterwards to be said'. Then Jack arranged for the hospital chaplain to sit with Desmond and offer him the Catholic last rites. It was clear he was ready, in his own words, to 'release my atoms to Mother Earth, Goddess Gaia'. Since they were not permitted by hospital authorities to remain overnight with him, the whole family went out for dinner at one of his favourite restaurants, toasting Desmond with champagne, as he had requested, and amusing each other with their reminiscences of him. Sammy remembers at one point in the evening glancing towards the door of the premises where 'I saw him standing there as a young man in his RAF uniform looking very handsome, and I knew he was going.' In fact, Desmond died early the following morning when once more the family called to see him in hospital. He had lapsed into a coma and as dawn broke on 24 February 2001 and the clouds cleared over the Baie des Anges, shafts of dazzling sunlight dramatically struck the Alpes Maritimes. At precisely that moment, Desmond died.

Obviously, given his esoteric beliefs, he was never going to receive a standard funeral but it took some time to overcome French bureaucracy and make alternative arrangements. Desmond had always made it clear that he did not wish to be embalmed – he believed this hindered the flight of the soul from the earthly body – and that he was to be laid out for three days to allow his spirit sufficient time to become free. The authorities, particularly hospital staff and the local police, had to be pacified and persuaded

Desmond's body laid out in French chapel St Salvator's, 2001.

the corpse should not be sent, as was usually the case, to a local undertaker. For the family, now joined by Wendyl's mother Jennifer Phipps who had arrived from Canada, achieving Desmond's last intentions seemed a hopeless task until an ally appeared in the form of one of his old friends, the Countess Ariane de Lalange. Turning up unexpectedly soon after the death, she declared that Desmond had summoned her from Paris. Discovering the Leslies' predicament, she offered her home in nearby Biot; its grounds contained a Romanesque chapel dedicated to St Julian and despite ongoing objections from the police, Desmond was eventually moved there after farcical scenes that saw his corpse slip and nearly disappear down a mountainside. In due course, dressed in his White Eagle robes and surrounded by candles, Desmond was laid out as he had requested and watched over by his extended family. 'It was a very beautiful three days,' remembers Sammy. 'The way death should be, very happy and very moving.' More champagne was drunk, more stories told, more tears shed. During this time, Mark and his uncle Jack visited St Salvator's, the local family church where they happened to meet the hospital chaplain who had given Desmond the last rites. He was able to provide reassurance that the deceased had received these in a suitable frame of mind. At the end of the three days, the body was cremated in Grasse. A week later, back in Ireland a memorial service was held in the local Catholic church and on 29 June, when Desmond would have turned eighty, the family organized a birthday party at Castle Leslie.

Obituary notices tended to remember the more sensational aspects of Desmond Leslie's life such as his authorship of *Flying Saucers Have Landed*, his complex personal relationships and the televised assault on Bernard Levin. *The Independent*, for example, described his history as rivalling 'any fiction by Nancy Mitford or Anthony Powell, with overtones of a Fifties sci-fi movie, and a little Weimar decadence thrown in'. Among the general public, there are two groups who continue to admire Desmond's achievements: believers in UFOs, who hold his work in this area during the 1950s in high esteem; and admirers of avant-garde music who avidly collect recordings of musique concrete. Plenty of internet sites – where he is often known as 'Des Les' – celebrate his work in one or other of these fields. But his fiction is little known today and so too is most of his work on world religions, except insofar as the latter connects with theories of alien landings.

Filmed for a television documentary in April 1996, Desmond – by then almost seventy-five – commented that he had enjoyed a wonderful life, 'and I hope we made the most of it'. As far as his family and friends were concerned, all the evidence pointed towards Desmond having made the most of his time on this earth. In retrospect, they remember his humour, his vitality, his enthusiasm and charm. Although relations with his children were at times stormy, eventually they were all reconciled to their father. 'As a grown-up,' remembers Antonia, 'he was one of my best friends to the very end. He could turn a rainy afternoon into an entertainment so you didn't know where the time had gone. I couldn't help but adore him – I just loved his company.' But their memories are tinged with a sound awareness of Desmond's flaws. 'He'd a messy life,' accepts Mark Leslie, 'and he didn't achieve his full potential. But he did manage to save Glaslough.' Ultimately, even if insufficiently celebrated, this was Desmond Leslie's greatest accomplishment: that in the face of considerable odds and contrary to expectations he preserved his much-loved family home. Devoting himself to the task meant other ambitions – as a writer and composer – had to take second place. They suffered accordingly; it is only necessary to compare Desmond's creative output in the 1950s with that of the following decade to appreciate the impact made by Castle Leslie on his time and energy. It is, of course,

All Desmond's children gathered for the first time when he died, 2001.

impossible to say what he might have achieved had he remained in London but Desmond knew that by returning to Ireland he had sacrificed certain opportunities. 'It is sad,' says Sammy, 'that he didn't live another year to see Castle Leslie hit centre stage internationally with the wedding of Paul McCartney and Heather Mills. Dad had helped record music for the Beatles in the early years of Abbey Road.' While this was a matter of some disappointment, Desmond never regretted the decision taken in 1963 nor the years of struggle that followed. Nor should he have done so. Thanks to the choice he made then, Castle Leslie remains in the possession of his family. That is Desmond Leslie's ultimate, and greatest, legacy.

Personal Recollections of Desmond Leslie

Young Master Desmond

Jack Leslie

Brother Desmond was born four years after me and six years after my sister Anita. He was a caesarian baby, and I remember a message being sent up the speaking tube in our nursery at 10 Talbot Square, London: 'A little brother has been born for Master Jackie.' Anita was cross and said, 'Why not for me?'

Nanny Watson took control and came to Glaslough with us for the summer. I soon discovered that if I said 'Buzz' to Desmond in his pram he had fits of hysterical laughter and wet his pants. So I kept saying 'Buzz' until I was forbidden to say it. We had now moved to 12 Westbourne Terrace, London. Desmond went to Gladstone's day school in Kensington and I was sent to an English prep school on Lake Geneva, while Anita remained at home with our governess Miss Overy. At that time Desmond got seriously ill with rheumatic fever and remained delicate for the rest of his life. Then he went to

Lady Cross Catholic boarding school in Sussex. He was very happy there and I remember visiting him with our mother and walking over the high cliffs of Beachy Head. Many of his friends went on to Ampleforth so he chose to go there.

Meanwhile, in 1929, Mother had bought a little, probably medieval, cottage, at Bendish, a tiny village between Hitchin and Luton in Hertfordshire. Only thirty miles from London, there was no electric light and water came from a well 300 feet deep. Bendish was situated between the vast estate of the Jack Harrisons at King's Walden, which employed twelve gamekeepers dressed in green uniforms, and Lord and Lady Strathmore's beautiful Queen Anne house at St Paul's Walden.

This was still the 'old' England and many of the inhabitants of Bendish had never been to London. Smith was our gardener and lived in a house in the village where his wife kept chickens. The Smiths spoke with a local accent and talked about 'hoak trees' and 'hash trees'. Desmond gave a firework display in the orchard to amuse the village children. I remember mothers saying to their children, 'If you don't behave you'll get a good 'iding.' One evening the Jack Harrisons gave a ball for one of their nine daughters. We set out in full evening dress, thinking Smith and the Summerbers, who ran the local pub, would be impressed by our finery, but all they did was hold their sides with laughter.

Desmond enjoyed Ampleforth and when we visited him he guided us all over the wild Yorkshire moors and to the ruins of Byland and Rievaulx Abbeys. When I was at Magdalene College, Cambridge, Mother and Desmond came to visit and we rowed on the river Cam under the bridges of 'The Backs'.

Being four years younger, Desmond missed the unending debutante balls given from May to August during the London season, except for one he attended with me at Lady Londonderry's Londonderry House. In July 1938, with war getting closer, it was the last great ball at Londonderry House, which later became an Airforce Club.

When I joined the Irish Guards, Desmond would visit me at the Tower of London and Wellington Barracks. Having left Ampleforth, he started going to the Café de Paris and other nightclubs and bringing home pretty girls for tea with Mother at her charming flat in South Lodge, Grove End Road.

Then came the outbreak of war in May 1940. I was captured by the Germans. Desmond wrote me letters and sent me family photos while I was a POW and on my return in May 1940 fondly embraced me. He had joined the RAF. After the war he had difficulties with Agnes and married Helen. Helen and Desmond invited me to her pretty little villa at St Jeannet and we used to go for drives up into the surprisingly wild mountains with beautiful wooded valleys and old villages perched on hilltops.

To my sorrow he left the Catholic Church and joined the White Eagle Lodge. Then he began to attend services and witnessed spirit materializations. He once told me that a Red Indian girl appeared. I asked him if he touched her. 'Yes,' he said 'she felt like a blown-up balloon.' He also made friends with George Adamski and they both came to visit me at my house in Rome. I felt suspicious of Adamski when he would not enter the little church of St Benedetto in Piscinula next to my house. I got more suspicious when he said he had just had an interview with Pope John XXIII. The Pope was actually dying and could not receive anyone.

Although his heart was always at Glaslough, the Mediterranean climate was better for Desmond's emphysema and he enjoyed French wine and food. He was keen on prayer and meditation and used to quote Mahomet's saying: 'The sun is the shadow of God.'

Desmond Leslie and God
Sean Leslie

DESMOND LESLIE and GOD

Desmond died in 2001, Cap D'Antibes.
Before he died, with great happiness he told Mark:
"This is the most exciting day of my life".
I think I can explain this.
Desmond had always been troubled by the fact
that he had been refused Holy Communion at the local
church by the priest on the grounds that he had married Helen
and had Sammy and Camilla.
I was talking with him one day shortly before he died
and he told me this; "God showed me a vision of
himself and me, me like a speck of soot circling the sun,
and God as the sun himself. I was tempted to despair,
so small and wicked did I feel, but God told me:
"Look at it my way." Desmond got into the mind
of the Sun, and saw that from God's point of view
He was enlightening him, not judging him for being
a speck of soot.
               Desmond cheered up and died shortly afterwards.

                              Sean
                              —

Writers Should Never Have Children

Sammy Leslie

When one of us six got up to tricks, my father would often tease that 'writers should never have children', and we would often tease back that writers were not fit to have them. The irony is that most of his children have become writers or wordsmiths in various forms.

Light-hearted as the banter was, the story behind it was more hurtful and took place when Dad was about five years old. He was sitting at the bottom of the nursery stairs of the castle and his father, 'the great and Glorious Sir Shane', swept past. He stopped and turned, looked down his long hooked nose at the child and demanded, 'Who are you, little boy?' Dad managed to squeak, 'Master Desmond,' and Shane tutted, and turning on his heel muttered, 'Writers should never have children.'

It must have hurt Dad to the core. Even though he often laughed about it and was a larger than life character, I think that much of his vulnerable side, which I saw in later years, came from his Victorian upbringing. I stayed with him a couple of weeks before he died and he retold the story with a quiver in his voice that betrayed the hurt he still felt.

It's amazing to look back at his childhood and how he was raised, and then to look at how differently my siblings and friends raise their children. The thought of showing affection or of loving a child unconditionally was unheard of for many parents, like Dad's, who were products of the Victorian ethos. The emotional vocabulary we are all so familiar with today was not even recognized let alone understood. To show emotion was seen as weakness, especially in a man, something to which the female of the species was unfortunately susceptible but not to be encouraged. The irony is that what was often thought of as a very privileged upbringing was sometimes everything but, in the true sense of what a child needs.

Given Dad's own childhood and the fact that I was number five in the line, what he lacked in the odd skill he more than made up for in other ways. I was probably the closest child to him, not because he favoured any of us over another, but because he mellowed in his fifties and we shared a great love of horses, of the land and trees and of the estate itself. Even as a child, I knew in my heart that I would, in time, take up the reins here.

He gave me a great sense of perspective and an understanding that true privileges are not measured in terms of wealth or the size of your house, but in terms of an open mind and heart. A curiosity about the world and how people think, and how we are all looking for the same things: to love and be loved and accepted for just being us. For me, the real privilege was sitting at the dinner table, where even as children we were encouraged to have healthy debates and to hear and respectfully challenge the views of others. Growing up right on the border during the Troubles gave me a balance in a place where some people hated others simply because they were of a different faith or belief.

I went to visit Patrick Moore recently. He and Dad were firm old friends even though they fundamentally disagreed over the existence of flying saucers. They debated heavily with one another, which, if anything, only seemed to strengthen their bond. Dad taught me to understand the core teachings of different faiths around the world and that they are often the same, and how they were frequently hijacked over the centuries to suit the ruling classes in war and peace. He taught me to understand the difference between religion and spirituality and to look for the core of what was being said or taught. The biggest sins we could commit in his eyes were to be cruel, bigoted, narrow-minded or Boring. As far as he was concerned, only boring people ever got bored, and there was a huge life out there waiting to be explored and lived to the full.

We spent an amazing time with him in France when he passed over; we all got to say our goodbyes and spend time with him afterwards. During three days in the mountains and in that tiny chapel we shared our experiences of his colourful life. He also taught me that if you sit quietly in a calm place and think of someone you love, who has died, you can often feel the warmth of their presence and hear their gentle voice. Nine years later, he feels closer than ever.

Coming Full Circle
Wendyl Jay

I find it interesting how Desmond's life came full circle. A lesson in synchronicity. Desmond was larger than life to me. When I first saw him at the Watervliet New York train station, it was like something out of a movie: the steam from the engine surrounding him in his black cape; my youngest sister, Milly, in tow. He was my father, the part of the picture I had not yet met. Years later I was invited to 'return' to Castle Leslie with my sons, Aaron and Matthew, his oldest grandchildren. I was thirty-eight. The moment my feet touched the ground, I knew this was home. For the first time, I understood why I felt things a bit differently than most. Without consciously knowing, I had followed much the same spiritual path as my father.

Over the years I have returned to the castle, growing more confident in who I am and my place in this family. 'There is much to learn and little time,' Desmond would say. We shared so much: our love of music and our understanding of UFOs. I spoke to fairies and had dreams; I naturally felt the ley lines and talked to dead people. I was a witch. 'A certified, card-carrying, all-American witch!' Desmond said to the local Catholic priest visiting from Glaslough, at Aggie's memorial. I shared his humour. Most importantly, I shared his spirit.

One of my most poignant memories is of the time of his crossing. I had always thought it would be amazing to see my mother and father together, call it an 'adopted' child's wish. When it became apparent that Desmond would soon be leaving this realm, I called my mother, Jennifer. She was on the next flight from Canada to say her farewells but did not arrive in time, at least not in this world. We had gone to our hotel for the evening for a bit of sleep. As I slumbered just before the dawn, I had a dream I saw my mother and father, Jen and Desmond, having a quiet dinner in a restaurant. They were at the age when they had met and become lovers. He was tall, handsome, charming; she gentle, kind and beautiful. They truly shared a love. I was not conceived yet, but I knew this must have been the moment where I, as spirit, chose them to be my blood parents. The ratta-tat-tat knock on my hotel room door woke me. 'Desmond has passed, we must go to the hospital.' As I lay there, clearing my head, the reality of the gift I had just received set in. The bits and pieces of my life fell into place and I understood love and all its capabilities. There is another space from which we come and go. A place from which we make our decisions and choices. The brethren from White Eagle Lodge had sent a message to be whispered into Desmond's ear as he journeyed to the other side: 'There is no separation.' Perhaps there is no greater wisdom.

Last Child by Last Mother

Camilla Leslie

The most obvious thing to say about my father is that I wish he were still alive. I believe I'm now mature enough to appreciate him. Our half-century age gap meant our 'needs' often didn't meet; I needed a traditional father and he needed a non-traditional daughter. I wish I could share my life's 'achievements' with the man who made me. He'd love that I write screenplays. He'd love his grandson, Paolo Luca. He'd love that I'm getting more eccentric by the hour. And he'd love that I live in the south of France beside my mother Helen, in the place where he spent his final years.

My happiest memory of my father was when he took me to Disney for my thirteenth birthday. Off we jetted to stay in a friend's luxury Floridian hotel. The owner's son was called Bobby, his wife Pamela. I was a Dallas addict. This was all too much. We borrowed an outrageous pale-green convertible Cadillac and every day we drove to a different theme park. We went on every 'whizzer', as Dad used to call them.

Embarrassing then was the infamous letter my father wrote to my Dublin boarding school. Aged fifteen, three other students and I decided to sell our subsidized tickets to Lansdowne Road (for an Ireland rugby match) for a small 'fortune', and buy six litres of cider to drink in a car park. We were suspended from school. My parents were in France and I was fearful that I'd be in huge trouble but in true character Dad decided to sue the school (suing was a favourite sport of his) and, much to my headmaster's fury, deduct six weeks of fees.

On a sad note, Jasper, my adored Dachshund, accidentally met an early grave under Dad's car. Daddy couldn't speak about it without crying and I never managed to speak about it with him at all. It put an extra barrier between us. But twenty years later, on my fortieth birthday, a Dachshund puppy suddenly appeared in my life. He had already been christened Peter (Dad's middle name) and was born on the same date that Dad died. Pure coincidence? Probably. But a part of me likes to think of it as some sort of delightful celestial connection.

Dad 'forgot' to tell my mother, away at the time, that I had made my Holy Communion and had changed to the Catholic school midterm. I was desperate to be the same as everyone else back then, especially my village 'guru', Brenda. And Catholic Daddy was all for it but didn't tell Protestant Mommy. I got a lovely new white dress, shiny sandals, a bible 'to read', a white lacy veil and little white handbag. After the ceremony Dad suggested I go up to the bishop and ask for a blessing. Ever the entrepreneur I did just that. And in my best Monaghan accent and with hands on hips, I also asked him for '50p'. Daddy roared with laughter.

Not long afterwards I was watching TV with 'normal' people in a 'normal' house. Bliss. Suddenly a clip came on screen. And a man, looking suspiciously like my father, whacked another man in the head. My heart sank. I foresaw complete ostracism. But luckily no one recognized Dad hitting Bernard Levin on the That was the Week That Was show. Now I beam with pride when people tell me that it's one of their favourite pieces of TV footage.

When Dad wasn't storming out of the castle he was meditating in his temple, badly located above the kids' TV room. I remember the utter embarrassment when friends were over and there'd suddenly be a 'ghostly' thumping on the ceiling telling us to keep quiet. I just didn't 'get' his need for spiritualism in my youth. He tried to interest me with child-adapted books on White Eagle. The pictures of suns and fairies were cute but couldn't compete with my Bunty, Tammy or Jinty magazines.

The most wonderful gift my father ever gave me was freedom of speech and thought. He never censored. He put up no metaphorical ceilings. Life was what you wanted it to be. I struggled with this as a child and yearned for more guidance and clearer boundaries. I wasn't ready then for such an open world. But I would not be the person I am today, taking the risk to write, without his eternal unspoken blessing and support. I can easily forgive that I needed to remind him who I was when I telephoned.

'It's child number six from mother number three, Daddy.'

'Ah, Milly darling!'

A small price to pay for being allowed 'to be'. A very precious gift from a father to his last child.

First Meeting With Desmond

Herbie Brennan

We (my publisher Norman Ames and I) held a weekly meeting, ostensibly so I could tell him, editor to publisher, my plans for magazine content. In fact these meetings – and many an unnecessary business lunch and car trip – were a vehicle for him to put forward his own ideas. To be fair, he never pulled rank or insisted on anything, but when he was really interested in an idea, he would sell it to me endlessly until I (usually) gave in from sheer exhaustion. Some of his suggestions were stupid, like his notion for an article entitled 'Green Means Stop', about the Irish habit of halting at green traffic lights while driving through the red. Others actually excited me, like the time he suddenly announced that I should run an interview with Desmond Leslie.

Back in the early 1950s, Desmond Leslie collaborated with a Polish-American named George Adamski on a book called *The Flying Saucers Have Landed*. I picked up the paperback while I was working in the *Lurgan Mail*. The opening section, by Adamski, was a first-person account of how, in November 1952, he met a spaceman from Venus who had landed his flying saucer in the Californian desert. It was this account that generated the book's title and turned it into a best-seller, but despite affidavits from several witnesses, I found Adamski's story unlikely. The second section, by Desmond Leslie, was something else. Without comment on Adamski's claims, Leslie produced an exposition of flying saucer sightings throughout history, tracing the phenomenon to ancient times, inserting the occasional esoteric reference and diverting to consider such mysteries as how the pyramids were built. His guided tour of the *Mahabharata*, one of India's two major Sanskrit epics, was especially interesting. Leslie interpreted it as an account of a prehistoric war that used flying saucers (called *vimanas*), laser weapons and atomics.

More to the point, he quoted from his sources, allowing readers to see for themselves the passages on which he based this unorthodox interpretation. Leslie wrote with a light touch and a relaxed style. Where Adamski sounded like a nut, he came across as a serious author. His ideas about a technically advanced prehistoric civilization fascinated me to such a degree that, many years later, I wrote four books of my own on the subject. But I knew nothing of Leslie himself. On the basis of his literary voice and a few hints dropped within the text, I believed him to be a retired army colonel living somewhere in England.

'Is he visiting Ireland?' I asked Norman.

'He's living in Dublin,' Norman said. 'I've been in touch with him and he's quite amenable to an interview. If you're interested, of course.'

I didn't even pretend to be irritated at the editorial interference. 'I'm interested,' I said.

'Will you send Hilary or do the interview yourself?'

Hilary was Hilary Weir, a staff trainee prone to disappearing for entire afternoons at a time. When I challenged her about it, she told me she had been attending sessions of the Dáil to sharpen her sense of civic responsibility. 'I'll do it myself.'

'Be careful what you ask him,' Norman told me casually. 'He knocked down Bernard Levin on TV.'

Although it seemed as unlikely as Adamski's Venusian, I quickly discovered it was true. Levin had apparently written a bad review of a stage performance by Leslie's wife, the actress Agnes Bernelle. Shortly afterwards, Leslie walked out of the audience at one of Levin's TV talk shows, invited him to stand up and punched him in the face. A surprised Levin fell over, but was able to continue the show minutes later.

'The irony is,' said Norman, who always claimed he disliked gossip, 'he's now left his wife for another woman. That's why he's living in Dublin.'

I don't know how Bernard Levin felt when Desmond towered above him, but he certainly put the wind up me. Standing in the doorway of his Terenure flat, he looked like a giant; and at six foot four he very nearly was. I decided to avoid controversial questions. The flat had a temporary feel about it. He showed me into a large living area with cables snaking across the carpet to link into a featureless black box lying in the middle of the floor. A statuesque blonde, herself easily six-foot tall, rose to greet me. 'This is Helen,' Desmond said. 'My other wife.'

'He has two,' Helen told me confidentially and grinned. 'Would you like a glass of wine?'

The wine took the edge off any formality and we were soon chatting like old friends. I didn't quite know what to make of Desmond. He had a rolling, plummy, English accent and the same turn of phrase that had marked him as a retired colonel in his book, but from his conversation he seemed to be Irish and there was nothing of the military about him. He wore large black-rimmed glasses and walked with steps so tiny I wondered if he might suffer from a disease of the legs. Helen was easier. 'Desmond rescued me from the orgy set in Chelsea,' she told me cheerfully. Desmond nodded benignly. 'She was a very naughty girl.' I noticed, with some trepidation, that there was a school cane hanging from a hook in the ceiling.

Desmond told me he was a composer and we listened to some of his compositions on tape. He specialized in 'musique concrete', an abstract form for which there was something of a fashion in intellectual circles at the time. I listened without appreciation or understanding, but, mindful of Levin's fate, kept criticisms to myself. 'Did you hear that?' Desmond asked as a very curious sound insinuated itself into the piece. 'I got that by farting in the bath.'

Sometime in the middle of the afternoon I realized I'd been drinking too much wine and asked if we could do the interview. It lasted three and a half hours and took some interesting turns. We began, predictably, with flying saucers, but diverted when I asked him how he reconciled Adamski's Venusian story with the findings of the recent space probe, which showed the planet had a sulphuric acid atmosphere and a surface temperature hot enough to melt lead. Desmond told me that 'as a student of theosophy' he had never believed the physical plane of Venus would be habitable, but that sentient human life existed there 'on the etheric plane'.

I pricked up my ears when I heard the word 'theosophy' and thereafter – apart from one brief interlude when Desmond claimed to have invented Patrick Moore – the interview concentrated on such esoteric matters as the Stanzas of Dzyan, the Christian Mysteries, levitation, mediumistic dematerialization and the Ark of the Covenant, which Desmond believed to be 'a highly sophisticated piece of electrostatic equipment'. I was in my element and could not get enough of it, but I was also aware that much of what interested me most would be obscure in the extreme to *Scene* readers, so I reluctantly brought the focus back to flying saucers. If one came down in the Phoenix Park, I asked, what would the reaction be? 'Depends who saw it first,' said Desmond. 'If it was Dev, he'd trip over it. If it was the Papal Nuncio, he'd spray it with holy water. If it was the American Ambassador, he'd probably try to buy it.' It was the perfect sign-off for my feature.

'Would you like to stay for supper?' Helen asked as I switched off my recorder.

'Yes, please,' I said.

I can no longer remember the meal, except that it was followed by some very runny Brie – the first I had ever tasted. While we were eating, I asked casually, 'What's that black box in the middle of the floor?'

'It's a flying saucer detector,' Desmond said.

'And the cane hanging on the hook?'

'Ah,' Desmond said. 'That's to keep this one –' he nodded towards Helen '– in her place.' He looked at me sleepily. 'Would you like a demonstration?'

Before I could answer, Helen jumped up and bent over. She was wearing a leather mini-skirt and looked very fetching. Desmond took the cane from the hook and whacked her soundly across the bottom. 'Ow, that hurts!' she protested.

'That's the whole point,' Desmond told her.

They returned to the table and Helen passed me the Brie.

The interview led to friendship. I became a frequent visitor to Desmond Leslie's Terenure flat. We spent hours discussing theosophy, magic and religion. All three were intimately entangled in Desmond's head. He still considered himself a Roman Catholic, albeit one with unorthodox ideas, but told me the Catholic Mass was a magical ceremony that had lost its way. The problem, as he saw it, was that priests (except for Jesuits) no longer had the visualization training that would allow them to work the rite with real magical power. 'I have only ever seen it done properly in the Liberal Catholic Church,' he said thoughtfully. 'When those towering archangelic forms came roaring in, it sent a shiver down my spine.'

'How come you mentioned Jesuits?' I asked curiously.

He looked at me in surprise. 'Haven't you read the *Spiritual Exercises of St Ignatius*? They're exactly the same training a magician receives.'

I hadn't, but I soon did and discovered he was right: when you stripped away the Christian elements, the *Spiritual Exercises* bore a striking resemblance to the training I was undergoing with Helios.

It was a relief to find someone with whom I could share my esoteric interests so openly. Despite her spiritualist leanings, Helen did not really approve of magic (which she considered dangerous) so I avoided discussions with her. Norman, to my surprise, had proved sympathetic when I made a tentative confession, but only really wanted to talk about how magical visualization might get him money. Desmond, by contrast, was open to everything that interested me, plus more besides, and had many more years experience in the field. At the time, I sometimes found him credulous and simplistic. Now, looking back, I am astounded to discover how profoundly he influenced my thinking on a wide range of subjects, and how much he knew about them.

During our discussions, I learned he had more time for spiritualism than I had – like Helen he was a member of the White Eagle Lodge. Despite my visionary experience in the séance with Eileen Boyd, I had never witnessed any objectively spectacular phenomena. Desmond, however, claimed he had: at a séance conducted by 'the materializing medium, Harris'.

The materializing medium Harris was Alexander Frederick Harris, a Welsh spiritualist who died in 1974, six years after my conversation with Desmond. Harris was brought up a conventional Christian and remained so until his sister Connie died. The grieving family attended a séance held by the Scottish medium, Helen Duncan, who conjured up Connie's spirit form. The young Alec was so impressed he decided to develop his own spiritual gifts and eventually claimed to have succeeded in materializing Connie himself.

For commercial séances at his home in the Whitchurch area of Cardiff, Harris permitted himself to be tied hand and foot to a chair in an open cabinet. The room was lit by the same sort of red photographer's light I'd seen used by Mr Sludge. Spirit forms materialized within the cabinet and walked into the room where they would talk with sitters. This was the type of set-up popularized by America's Davenport Brothers in the mid-nineteenth century. Since one of them admitted to Harry Houdini that their séances were fraudulent – essentially an escape act masquerading as spiritualism – it was not a set-up that inspired confidence. Certainly it inspired little confidence in Desmond: 'When the so-called spirits appeared I could hardly believe Harris had been getting away with such a crude deception. They clumped about the place in hobnailed boots. They were obviously accomplices dressed up.'

He decided to expose the fraud. Although sitters had been warned before the séance that they must not under any circumstances try to touch the spirits, Desmond leaped from his seat and grabbed one by the arm. 'I was never so surprised in my life. The creature simply dissolved under my hand and disappeared.'

Helen Strong, who was listening to the account, nodded. 'That's right – I watched it happen.'

Since it seemed a good time to swap phenomena stories, I told Desmond of my encounter with the miniature horses at Longstone Rath. He listened without comment until I had finished, then said, 'But dear boy, don't you know what those were?' I didn't and said so. 'Those were *faerie* horses,' he told me soberly. 'They're associated with the raths of Ireland and also with Japan.'

On one occasion while searching for a reference book, he pulled an old photograph from a drawer. 'That's Castle Leslie,' he said. The photograph was blurred and seemed to show an old country house. Since he always claimed to be broke, I assumed the designation 'castle' was another example of Desmond's humour, but it subsequently turned out there really *was* a Castle Leslie and a 1200-acre estate.

'You must come and see it sometime,' Desmond said. Then added a little bitterly. 'If I ever get things sorted with Aggie.'